Economy Ecology & Kindness

Other books by Roy Gillett

Astrological Diaries 1978 to 1990
A Model of Health
Zen for Today's Living
The Essence of Buddhism
Astrology and Compassion the Convenient Truth
The Secret Language of Astrology
Reversing the Race to Global Destruction

Roy Gillett combines twenty years of experience in City of London business and school teaching with thirty more as an astrologer and Buddhist. He is President of Britain's *Astrological Association* and a past-Trustee of London's *Jamyang Buddhist Centre*. Since 1979, he has written many regular mundane astrology columns. From the 1990s he has guided users of the *AstroAnalyst* ground-breaking financial astrology software. Roy speaks for astrology at international conferences and on the media. All this experience has fuelled the extremely valuable insights this book offers.

In 2017 he wrote *Reversing the Race to Global Destruction*, a sequel to *Economy Ecology and Kindness*. See the end pages for more details of how to order this ten-years-on assessment of the world economy's progress.

Economy Ecology & Kindness

World Economy & Astro-cycles 1984-2024

What are the real causes and lasting solutions to our current crises?

by

Roy Gillett

Crucial Books

First published in 2009 by
Kings Hart Books

Second edition published 2018 by
Crucial Books
PO Box 1061, Camberley GU15 9PL
http://crucialbooks.co.uk/

A catalogue record for this book is available from the
British Library.

Book: ISBN 978-1-906154-15-8

E-booK: ISBN 978-0-9956999-0-8

Acknowledgements

Thanks to Astrolabe Inc [http:www.alabe.com] for use of *Solar Fire V7 Gold* and *AstroAnalyst* software to generate astrological and price charts, and to calculate the various dates and periods of the astro-cycles.

The work, wisdom and achievement of numerous devoted astrologers, financial market traders and analysts, Buddhist friends, planetary healers, and people of good will in all walks of life have been the inspiration that has driven this work. I hope that everyone who knows me will recognise the part they have played. Special thanks to Colin Shearing and Elizabeth Plant of Kings Hart Books for their generous and wise guidance through the publishing process.

As always the profoundly kind and tireless persistence of Lama Thubten Zopa Rinpoche continues to generate hope. Without Rinpoche's example and my wife Carolyn's untiring support my ability to offer these ideas would not have been possible and, in many other respects, the value of my life's endeavours would have been far less.

Important Note

Nearly all experimental studies have been unable to find a statistical relationship between a wide range of isolated astrological concepts and expected outcomes. However, since astrological concepts are interdependently variable, some scientists and most astrologers consider such tests to be inappropriate. Astrology is a symbolic language and offers a balance of probabilities rather than specific certainties. Bear this in mind and seek qualified professional advice for all medical, financial, legal and other specialist questions.

Contents

'Too much energy in your country is spent
developing the mind instead of the heart,
Be compassionate, not just to your friends, but
to everyone...Never give up'
HH Dalai Lama of Tibet

'May there be great prosperity and may
everything needed be easily obtained...
May everyone ... have only compassion and
love for each other in their mind streams.
And may they only benefit and never harm
each other.'
Lama Thubten Zopa Rinpoche

Preface

Watching on television the 9/11 destruction of the twin towers, while knowing the astro-cycles of the time, brought deep foreboding to the minds of contemporary astrologers.

They could see it would need incredible wisdom to avoid breakdown in the United States' relationships and finances[1]. Imminent astro-cycles suggested over-reaching delusions of grandeur. Without wise restraint, political leaders could use the 9/11 events as an excuse to justify imperial adventures based upon misconceived over-optimism[2]. What happened is well known[3].

The worst did not have to happen

Particularly sad is that such worst-case scenarios can be avoided. Astrologers are only like Cassandra, cursed with foreknowledge of events that cannot be altered, for as long as they and the astro-cycles are ignored. Humanity has free will, but wise and selfless objectivity is needed to be able to see beyond the knee-jerk mood of the times, and then make proper use of it.

Ironically, those who ignore astro-cycles and insist on their 'freedom to choose' are those most likely to be at the mercy of events. Their actions are most predictable. We are especially vulnerable to behaving like this when we are hurt, and strike back automatically. Stopping, taking stock and asking why others acted as they did often clarifies and so heals the most unlikely situations. That many individuals and groups are resistant to doing so is a source of frustration and wonder to anyone who knows how astro-cycles work.

The tragedy of so many post-9/11 deaths and so much destruction, the breakdown of relationships, the waste of vast resources is that most could have been avoided. Those in power should have counselled against fear and revenge; not stirred up immature pride and personal glory. The opposition of Jupiter in Leo to Neptune in Aquarius did not have to be about egocentrically insisting we know best and bombing each other into surrender. This way, agreement never comes. Agreement comes when all sides question their beliefs and notions of self-importance.

Astro-cycles can prevent planning errors

When making economic decisions, considering astro-cycles with understanding and farsighted, positive motivation is equally valuable. By reacting to the cycles automatically with increasingly short-sighted greed, we experience inevitable booms and busts. Clever minds may find ways to distort and avoid the consequences of practical reality for a while. This will only make the correction, when it comes, all the more severe and difficult to understand and act upon.

The economic crisis that broke in 2008 is the result of our seduction and fall into the worst excesses of the astro-cycles of the times. Intrinsic shortcomings in our economic system enabled financial institutions to engage in risky unsustainable trades, driven by greed for personal gain. In the short term, everyone seemed to benefit from their actions. Our system was so unbalanced and fragmented that genuine cause and effect were hardly connected. Although seeming very practical, our 21st century physical world and business relationships are founded upon illusory values; driven more by sentiment, greed and fear than any real facts. Looking with genuine realism, we see they were doomed to fail.

The study that follows uses astro-cycles to explain why this is happening, could have been avoided and certainly can be avoided in the future.

Our reaction to astro-cycles creates our future

What happens in our lives is determined by how we respond to challenges. There are three possible levels. If a traveller meets a brute on the road, he can: surrender to the brute's will; devise a trick to hide and run away; or he can face and defeat the difficulty once and for all.

When applying this analogy to our economic challenges, there are three similar choices. We can protect what we have and blame and attack others, accusing them of causing our problems: join the brute. We can manipulate interest rates, money supply, extend debt, and seek to stimulate consumption in artificial and often unnecessary ways. Some elements of such short-term tricks may be needed to ease the transition to the third option. However, the real solution is to question assumptions that have brought us to similar predicaments for decades, even centuries. The economy is the way we manage material relationships. Because it is material, economic theory must follow the basic laws of physics — nothing is for nothing. Materials may change form, even from energy to mass, but nothing is intrinsically gained or lost.

Blinded by fear and greed, manipulated by pleasing media images of promised emotional and physical gratification, we have lost sight of the obvious. Those in power have misused the astro-cycle determined fashion of the time to manage our desires for their own benefit.

Now the astro-cycles have changed, all is ending in tears. This study uses the cycles to give a much deeper understanding of the past. It then explains those to come. The insight this offers will help us to control our destiny and enjoy a much better future.

Astro-cycles put the economic crisis in perspective. Our economic and ecological crises share a common solution. A truly sustainable economy has all interests working in harmony. Its only unit of exchange is based upon genuine giving and taking — a new "gold" standard based upon kindness.

Introductory
Considerations

Chapter 1
The Fundamental Financial Fact

'The key aim is to become richer and have more and more, whether we need it or not. Such motivation may work well while there is slack to take up. However, because it lacks self-regulation, what appears to be ever-expanding enjoyment of luxury is desperately temporary. Essentially, we remain no better than an advanced colony of ants consuming a very finite pile of sugar. Our methods of economic organisation, however brilliantly researched and implemented, are no more than stopgap ways of justifying unnecessary over-consumption to 'keep the show on the road'. **(Written 2005 to July 2007, published December 2007 when DJIA was at 13,780): Chapter 14 of** *Astrology and Compassion the Convenient Truth*[4].

The words and behaviour of the economists and political leaders handling the 2007-8-triggered economic crisis are fundamentally misguided. The world faces much more than a rare but natural downturn in the 'economic cycle', from which we will recover back to business as usual. We face radical change.

Economic crisis creators have no true solutions
The errors that caused the crisis need to be clearly identified, but this is being avoided. It seems we lack the words to ask the right questions. Economists and political leaders point to a 'world economic downturn, beyond their control'. Yet, these governments, reserve bankers, business leaders and economists have held numerous meetings for many years. In exotic places throughout the globe they have planned and developed the world economy. They are right to say not a single one of them caused such monumental miscalculations. They all did it together! They are all responsible!

If so, perhaps we should ask

* 'If the G20 national leaders and their advisers controlling 85 per cent of the world economy have, with the immense resources and expertise at their disposal, created the current crisis should we trust them to guide us out of it?
* Before we embrace their solutions should we question the theories of economics and business practice, upon which the 'solutions' are based?
* Are such solutions reliable or mere pseudo-science?'

Ordinary people in their heart of hearts always knew that the world economic boom was too good to be true, but were too humble to say so. How could we possibly know better than people with luxuriant business premises and lifestyles?   Were they not advised by the most brilliant minds, highly educated and qualified experts — Doctors of Philosophy, Professors, Nobel Prize-winning economists? Politicians discussed detailed policy in depth, employing these and other experts to ensure the public interest was carefully considered. We were happy to allow large rewards, because everything seemed so complicated. We paid top fees for rigorous auditing methods. Every detail was examined. We were told this ensured the balance between income and expenditure was transparent. Regulators were employed to ensure the rules of good accounting and business practice were kept to. Anyone 'not qualified' was excluded. When in the company of such highly qualified expertise', it felt at times that we were not even qualified to advise ourselves!

We were happy to live in a world where such brilliant financial experts had found ways to create the magic of constant consumption and 'painless' ever-available credit. How advanced our modern world was, offering us ever-better homes, possessions and extravagant leisure activities!   How inconvenient that ecologists mentioned the eco-balance of the planet may be suffering! Of course, we would do something if we could possibly find the money and the time.

As amazement turns to anger, it becomes obvious that our inner doubts were correct all the time. We were not only ravishing the resources of the planet; at fault was our state of mind about everything. Nothing comes for nothing. However easy it is and rich you are, someone has to pay. To truly balance the books, the audit must be based upon a far deeper, non-selective notion of give and take than that found in modern accounting. We need to move beyond short-term return and self-interest to a profoundly grounded economy; based upon just and ethical give and take.

In Chapter 2 and for the rest of this study, we will consider cycles that underlie far more than the ups and downs of the financial ones. These anticipate changes in our short-term assumptions about what is true. They help us plan by offering insight into how such changes will unfold. Firstly, however, we need to be clear about exactly what is and is not the fundamental financial fact.

Intrinsically flawed economic theory and practice

As we seek ways to restore global balance, it would help to question the content of modern business degrees and theories. Are these any more than devices to perpetuate and manipulate the cut and thrust of a thousands-of-years-old greed-based battle over resources? How different is a Stone Age hunter with a spear to an Enron trader manipulating supply to increase price, or a bonus-seeking trader mis-selling a loan? How different to banditry are creative accounting methods that pass on risk, give advantage, exploit, manipulate and delay the inevitable moment of truth for as long as possible? The mentality that bends and twists the rules for personal advantage not only cannot be trusted. It creates a mentality where no one can be trusted — everybody lies and distorts. We have seen many major world financial institutions covering their tracks to create and market sub-prime debt, 'supported by' helplessly exposed credit default swaps. Tempted by great material rewards, the several generations' brightest minds have been corrupted into building a complex, illusory, interdependent and empty 'emperor's-new-clothes' world economy.

Of course, only the extent of what has happened is new. The mundane world of business has always been a struggle between honest investors seeking to encourage the enterprise of conscientious workers against those who wish to trick something-for-nothing out of the process. Booms and busts occur, when the tricksters become the 'respected' leaders and more and more people seek to follow their lead. This early 21st century aberration is only more worrying than any before because of its extent and the standing of those who have led the deception. It is all the more worrying because it seems many of our business and political leaders who are responsible thought that they were acting with the best of intentions. The methods of manipulative accounting had become so advanced and the temptations so extensive that it really did seem boom and bust had at last been defeated. Everyone in the world could in time be rich and happy — once technology had solved the ecological consequences. Many of these people were not bandits seeking to rob the poor, but naïve, well-intentioned people caught out of their depth in self-delusion.

It is important to acknowledge this, not to 'rub salt into the wound', but to help us decide what to do next — especially to decide the right fundamental questions to ask and who to listen to for answers. Ironically, because the situation seems so serious and desperate this is the last thing we are likely to do. In the year from August 2007 and even more so in the months from September 2008 into 2009, those who presided over the creation of the crisis in the first place have insisted they are the experts to solve it. They have reacted with one hastily-applied knee-jerk action after another. When such measures did not show immediate results in propping up institutions and stimulating confidence, others were tried. They are repeating the same short-term economic strategy that created the problem. It is digging us into ever deeper medium - and long term – 'holes'. We have to stop making matters worse, think and determine just what is the fundamental financial fact? Then, we may see a way to plan properly.

'Solutions' that will not work

The main thrust of the G20 solutions tried to date centre around two concepts — regulation and stimulation.

* *Regulation* The irresponsible greed and self-interest of the key players causing the crisis have led to such anger that we are in danger of being distracted into expressing counterproductive retribution by means of intensive future regulation. After 9/11 intrusive surveillance regimes were put in place. These took away the liberty of ordinary people, but were just a new set of obstacles for the real perpetrators to work around. Today, new financial checks and balances and actions to curtail avoidance into offshore havens may give some protection. It may tidy up issues that governments have wanted to tackle for some time. It will also give profitable employment to specialists seeking new ways of avoidance. It will not, however, change aims and attitudes. It will just adjust the framework within which we practice to deceive each other.

* *Stimulus* For the government rescue packets to work without leaving a ruined debt-ridden world economy, there has to be a recovery of the kind that occurred from 1995 to 2000 and led to the Clinton budget surplus at the end of his last term. A repeat of what happened then is hoped for, with bank stock prices returning some of the way towards their 2007 levels. Then, what are at present bad assets can be sold back to the market at a profit and so enrich public exchequers. With interest rates near zero and central banks printing money, it is doubtful that this can be done without creating inflation that wipes out the real value of savings. The resultant deprivation suffered by

ordinary people and poor nations could lead to major social disruption.

Elements in this twin-pronged approach are to be welcomed as a short-term, stop-gap strategy to ease the pain millions of ordinary people are suffering, due to decisions over which they had no control. However, if this is all we do in the medium to long term, it will lead to counterproductive avoidance of the fundamental problem. A real solution needs to answer two central questions. Why do we need to be regulated? Do we 'answer' anything by being stimulated to consume? Surely, we have had enough of both!

This is the fundamental financial fact

Before we apply such Keynesian 'solutions'; look again at monetarist, market-based or even Marxist alternatives; regulate; consider complex theories of balance sheets and formulas of relationships between various elements of business activity, employment, supply, demand, training, we need to be clear of one simple question. Why do we want to work so hard in the first place?

Why expend all this energy? The usual answers are: to eat, to be protected, to experience pleasure, be free of worry, to give such experiences to those closest to us. Then will come aspirations of personal pride or group loyalty. 'I want to be the best', spread this belief, serve my country.

Such powerful emotional needs lead to assumptions about reality which can be misconceived or even manipulated and corrupted. We can be persuaded to give to others our freedom to decide what we really want. We may take without counting the consequential cost. We can be spurred on by false and illogical emotional righteousness, triggered by marketing and political propaganda.

There is an antidote to this danger, which is easy to understand and apply. Ask why for thousands of years farmers rotated their crops? It was to put back into the soil what they had taken from it. Similarly, in any sustainable economic system, 'for anything we take, an equal amount must be given in some way'. This is the fundamental requirement, if we wish to live a successful and happy economic life. This is the **fundamental financial fact**.

All error, fear, feelings of deprivation and experiences of suffering emanate from not understanding or submitting ourselves to this principle. We want to criticise and attack others, because we feel they have taken something we value. All economic booms and busts arise because more and more people seek to gain without giving back. Wars arise because opponents feel each other is acting or gaining unfairly. We look down upon or hate others because they reject what we value. All such attitudes are caused by the breakdown of selflessness. They are put right by understanding the benefits of give and take.

In the 21st century we are becoming increasingly aware of the 'carbon footprint' our actions create and are seeking to reduce it. Far more extensive and lethal can be another footprint — the one created by everything each one of us does. The food we eat has been brought to our table by the suffering and even death of many different creatures. A single thrust of a spade can destroy many; driving a car at dusk kills thousands. Clearing an industrial site wipes out endless billions and trillions. Even healing our body from disease is at the expense of billions of creatures that infected us. Of course, most of these actions cannot be avoided if we are to survive. Yet, at least we can plan and live our lives to be conscious of the effect of our actions — not just celebrate, brag about, and glory in the prosperity of our scientific mastery. The Universe is not a blank canvas there solely for our expression. It is very crowded indeed. When we realise this, we will see why we have to take every action with extreme care.

Idealism is the only way to happiness

'What has all this idealistic stuff got to do with the hard headed cut and thrust of the business world?' - you may ask. 'Nothing much', if we wish to struggle in a world of constant anxiety, based on the sure knowledge that everyone we meet may lie and cheat and take advantage of our good nature. If we want to feel at war with all creatures from the smallest insect to every person and culture that does not support us. Failing to care for others will not change our lives if we want the horror of job losses, the consequent hardship and ill health to erupt suddenly upon us. If we wish to be manipulated and bullied, if we wish to be powerless and ignorant of what controls our destiny, then we can continue to do what we like. We can suffer disappointment, doubt and never know why.

Those that reject such a self-centred world for themselves and their families will seek a better way. The price is not high. If we wish to live clean, genuinely productive and happy lives, we need to give and take deeply and intelligently. We need to move beyond justifying the existence of an arms factory, because it creates jobs; polluting local residents, because doing nothing is 'good for my business'; taking advantage of the vulnerable, because they do not know how to complain. We must stop deceiving ourselves that we can ignore our business partners' human rights and employment abuses, because they supply the cheapest. We must reject rules and regulations that are easily circumvented or ignored. The more we accept cheating as part of life, in our business and social institutions, how we sell to each other, in the way we treat the underprivileged all over the world, the more we open doors to those cheaters and bring disaster in our own lives. However advanced our business qualifications and structures, however tight our regulations and however skilfully we hedge and derive our investment option, if we act to avoid giving and instead take unfair advantage, we will do no more than prepare the ground for the next disaster. When we stimulate an economy based on compromised principles, we merely stimulate one disaster after another.

For, in business as well as every other aspect of life, the more mindfully and genuinely we give of what we have and understand, the more we will receive. The more we are principled, trustful and encourage trust, give generously and make friends, the less we need to be regulated and manipulated for 'our own good'. A society that 'balances the books' on every level of its existence will become stronger and its citizens permanently happier.

To keep it that way, we have to be objective about the moods and fashions of the time. This is where astro-cycles come in. The rest of this book explains how.

Chapter 2
What Astro-cycles Can Tell Us

'Capricorn is the 10th house archetype and the 'managing director' of earthly affairs, because it is strong and realistic. From 2008, the Pluto-in-Sagittarius years could be seen as irresponsibly over-expansive. We may feel we have accepted what our scientists, economists and leaders have offered and told us far too easily.**(Written 2005 to July 2007, published December 2007 when DJIA was at 13,780): Chapter 14 of** *Astrology and Compassion the Convenient Truth.*

On several occasions[5], Mervyn King, the Governor of the Bank of England, justified his failure to anticipate the 2007-8 crisis by insisting vehemently that he could be expected to plan with the benefit of hindsight. Certainly he is right if he means his advisory committee is ill-equipped. All they have to make projections are mere mechanical checks and balances, regulations that are constantly being circumvented, and no means to anticipate consumer sentiment and major political events.

What astro-cycles can tell us
Fortunately however, as this study will demonstrate, astro-cycles offer ways to anticipate financial[6] and social change[7]. Alexander Ruperti[8] explains the cyclic structure and Richard Tarnas [9] gives copious and irresistible examples from a vast sweep of history. This chapter focuses upon the help astro-cycles can offer in the making of economic decisions. Newcomers to astrology will find the brief introduction to the main concepts in the Appendix helpful[10].

Astrologers can anticipate how societies will experience upheaval (Pluto [11]), fashion and belief (Neptune) and innovation (Uranus). We study Jupiter to find when and how opportunity is strong and Saturn to decide when and how to focus upon structuring and consolidation. As these planets change zodiac signs and interact with each other, social attitudes and experiences change. By synthesising these cycles, we can assess the likely outcome of their combined effect and anticipate the future. We shall see in Chapter 6 that a combination of Pluto in Jupiter's sign, Sagittarius, with Uranus and Neptune mutually receiving each other in Aquarius/Pisces created an illusion of endless global technological expansion. The transit of Pluto hovering across the cusp of Capricorn, while Jupiter was in that sign and the Aquarian rulers Saturn/Uranus were opposed in 2008, triggered the credit crisis and downturn.

In the chapters that follow, we shall see what politicians and economists thought they were discovering, learning and teaching were not permanent scientific economic truths. The past 30 years were not a breakthrough away from boom and bust, but just another delusion trapping us into an even more severe repeat performance. Theories are only good during the time that the fashion we assume to be constant gels with a current astrological cycle. By repeating in an exact predictable order, each astro-cycle gives a powerful indication of what is to come. This is the science of astrology. However, at each moment, the pattern of how the cycles *combine* is unique. Synthesising and interpreting the effect of the uniqueness is the art of astrology.

By illuminating, astro-cycles help us to choose

Astro-cycles do not indicate exact, automatic outcomes. Forecasting with them is rather like forecasting how people will be affected by the weather. On a cold day, some will dress up warm, other brave the elements. The most unfortunate are those who were caught out dressed unsuitably, because they did not know the forecast.

Astro-cycles suggest an atmosphere that inclines our dispositions. Because they incline rather than determine, the cycles allow choices. In the company of aggressive people, only the boldest will seek to fight. As the astro-cycles change, so we change to reflect their nature. At the same time, we reject the assumptions of previous cycles and the people that perpetrated them. As with other environmental influences, astro-cycles offer choices for good or ill. In times of plenty, we can eat well, but also preserve and store for leaner times. To eat well and not store inevitably leads to starvation and a fight for survival. To use astrology to take the wiser course allows us to relax and recharge our batteries when times are tough. With Pluto in Sagittarius, wise astrologers plan with the knowledge that Capricorn is next to come. So should wise societies and their leaders.

The information in this booklet is critically important because it shows that astro-cycles offer advance knowledge to plan with. They provide the hindsight that Mervyn King denies is possible. In 2000, there were six planets in Taurus while Uranus and Neptune were mutually receiving each other in Aquarius/Pisces. This suggested realism about technical stocks — a top to their 1995-2000 boom. The wise would not have taken pension holidays in the run up, but instead built sufficient funds. Read ahead and you will see lots of examples where astro-cycles clearly offered the chance to assess the strength and length of a development and/or to know when growth, contraction or changes of fashion were likely.

Because astro-cycles are the underlying key, what happens is neither chaotic nor dependent upon some 'holy grail' economic science of absolute truths. Quite the opposite! When we understand the nature and timing of astro-cycles we know our range of choices and the likely consequences of each course of action. Within the limitations of the irresistible flow of the cosmos, we have the same freedoms as does a skilful sailor on the ocean — no more, no less. If a captain places the side of his ship facing a tidal surge, all on board will drown. Similarly in the world economy, ignoring the astro-cycle tide leads to wrong choices. So we face the barriers and bad experiences explained and foretold in the chapters ahead.

With the majority using the astro-cycles to make the right choices, we could have had a much better past and certainly can enjoy the alternative of the happier future described in this study.

With the help of astro-cycles we can learn to give and take in the profoundest sense[12], by being aware of and planning for the changing times. If we do, we will never find ourselves with $44,000,000 worth of new unsold automobiles parked outside Los Angeles. We will not again employ the most brilliant minds to bully the public into believing in an 'economic miracle', and then claim we could not have foreseen the outcome of our stewardship, as the world moves from boom to bust in hardly a year.

Chapter 3
World Economic Failures before 1984

'Money is a good servant, but a poor master.'
Traditional saying

Chapters 4 to 6 will study the intrinsic nature of and astrological reasons for the rapid expansion in financial activity, price levels and apparent wealth between 1984 and 2008. This chapter sets the scene by considering the origins of today's trading system and how contemporary astro-cycles have always helped to indicate its failings.

The South Sea Bubble
In 1697, there was an early attempt in England to protect investors from rigged markets and insider dealings. Yet the questionable involvement of government members, including the then Chancellor of the Exchequer, in the South Sea Company, built in 1720 into an infamous boom and bust, known as the South Sea Bubble. The account of events [13], especially in this key year 1720, has an uncannily modern feel. Shares rose steeply from £128 in January to £1,000 by early August, only to retreat to £150 in September. The price inflation was driven up by large numbers of new and inexperienced investors, plus a craze of borrowing to buy shares. It was then driven back down by short selling.

The outer planetary focus for the year anticipated the story. The dominating aspect, an illusory Saturn/Neptune opposition in Taurus and Scorpio, struggled with unstable and unrealistic expectations indicated by Jupiter applying to conjunct Uranus in Libra at the price top. Pluto being in Virgo led to uncertainty about standards of decency.

Putting the present crisis in perspective
London Stock markets had a chequered history through the remainder of the 18th century. Then in 1801 the

London Stock Exchange was formally founded. The end of the war in Europe and the Industrial Revolution, especially transportation stocks gathering momentum, boosted the markets on both sides of the Atlantic.

The diagram shows US performance in 1789-2008.

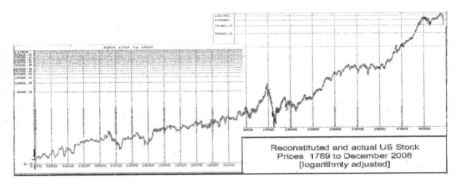

Reconstituted and actual US Stock Prices 1789 to December 2008 [logarithmly adjusted]

Due to inflation, plotting actual stock price average indices over long periods produces an almost flat line, with a slight rise and fall in 1926-1933 and then a dramatic rise during the last two decades of the 20th century. The diagram above is drawn logarithmically to allow for this price inflation. So, by looking at the steepness of the rise and fall line, we can compare business experiences that are decades or even centuries apart. We can see that the 1929 Wall Street Crash and the three years that followed were by far the worst downturn since records began in 1789.

At the time of writing, the 2008/9 downturn is far worse than October 1987, but not yet anywhere near as bad as 1929-33.   However, the upturn from the 1980s has been unrealistically steep, even in inflation-adjusted terms. In early March 2009, the Dow fell to a 12-year low of 6470 and then recovered. Many market analysts say that support at this level is weak. If it was to be tested again and breached, we could see a freefall back to 1994 or even 1980s levels.

Of course, the stock markets are just a part of the story. They merely anticipate what could lead to a dramatic downturn in what affects everyone's life —

demand, production and employment. To avoid repetition of life experiences reminiscent of the 1930s, a profound understanding of the causes and cures of the current malaise in the world economy is required. To enlighten our foresight, we can use astro-cycles to look back to the events surrounding not only the 1929 Crash, but also the Great Depression of 1835-42 — the modern industrial era's other major deflationary period.

Earlier major downturns in modern markets

With memory of the Napoleonic Wars fading into the past, by 1835 enterprise was booming and expectations were high. The year started with Jupiter in Gemini, Neptune just joining Uranus in Aquarius and Saturn in Libra completing a grand trine in air signs. Pluto in Aries was the immature, easy-going, happy-go-lucky outsider. Unfortunately, the expectations were just that — all in the mind and headstrong. In the seven years from 1835, US stock prices were to fall by nearly 80 per cent and the Second Bank of the United States (the approximate equivalent of the present Federal Reserve) was to become bankrupt. The astro-cycles moved on and now indicated relentless tension. In the last quarter of 1835 Jupiter, now in Cancer, squared Pluto twice. The following year it did so again and then went on to form a T-square between itself in Leo, Saturn in Scorpio and Neptune in Aquarius.

The graph shows the market price consequences. A recovery commenced from March 1843. Jupiter had joined Neptune in Aquarius for an incredibly rare period of multiple triple mutual receptions with Uranus in Pisces. It was off and on for two years. Afterward, prices flattened into the years of the Irish Potato Famine (1845-9), and then in the lead up to the American Civil War (1861-5). Only in the last years of the latter was recovery fully underway. In 1835, as 115 years earlier, the astro-cycles had stimulated an expectation and belief that growth was permanent; that a magic formula had been discovered. Ever-expanding economic prosperity in which more and more could share was at hand. Yet, as before, so much was to be lost by those who had expected to gain so much. By using knowledge of imminent change indicated by the astro-cycles, unrealistic expectation could have been tempered. Then unnecessary risk-taking would not have happened. Resources to navigate a way through those difficult years ahead could have been maintained and loss and starvation avoided.

As can be seen from the graph, the 1929 Crash and its aftermath were an even more dramatic economic change. After a difficult post-war adjustment, the second half of the Roaring Twenties saw investments booming ever upward. Borrowing to buy, trade and profit on the margin became the 'sensible' modern person's way of prospering. When reality struck and the non-sustainability of the markets became clear, the edifice upon which millions of peoples' lives was based came tumbling down. All was lost for vast numbers of people: firstly the investors and then the consumers and workers.

As dramatic as was this crash, so was the clarity of the astro-cycles predicting it. This time Uranus, not Pluto, was in impulsive Aries, encouraging the belief that the rules were changing. Neptune was in Leo — exactly opposite to its 1834-48 sign Aquarius. Fun and speculation were the fashion of the times. Pluto had been in Cancer since the beginning of World War I. Victorian values has been rejected. Previously accepted family structures and roles had been continually questioned! Now, however, fashion and the world picture were yet again to change.

The wise would have seen the writing on the wall when Neptune made its first entry into Virgo in September 1928. For the less wise its retrogression back into Leo in February 1929 offered 'reassurances' that the boom was 'permanent'. Then, in late July, Neptune completed its ingress into Virgo. The Leo (July/August) period passed without anxiety, as the inner planets trined and Jupiter sextiled Uranus in ever-positive Aries. However, as the inner planets moved through Virgo to Libra and opposed Uranus, no longer could practical reality be denied. The markets reacted on 13 October, when the Sun exactly squared Pluto and Mercury was four days before a direct station in exact opposition to the degree of Uranus. During the month that followed the Dow fell by 43 per cent in value. With Jupiter in Gemini holding back in retrograde, the price struggled to hold up at this lower level until July/September 1930, when Jupiter opposed Saturn across the Capricorn/Cancer axis and joined with Pluto to square Uranus in Aries. Triggered by Mars and ongoing opposition from Saturn, the Dow price continued to fall dramatically to a low below 41 on 11 July 1932 — a loss of 89 per cent from the 1929 high. It was not to recover to this 1929 high until 1954.

As in 1835, a wise economic planner would have seen through the ignorant blind attachment to easy gains. Knowing the astro-events described above were imminent would have provided the hindsight that Mervyn King determinedly denies is possible. A wise planner would have rejected the easy possibilities, realised assets and created reserves to resource the bad times. The world could have eased into a downturn, not crashed into disaster.

Lessons for today

There much to learn from these three examples, both in understanding the cause and finding the best way out of the early 21st century downturn. However, looking for exact mechanical relationships between planetary positions and events is unlikely to help. There is no simplistic repetition of particular planetary combinations as a 'boom/bust signal'. Rather, all three recessions show a common pattern in the way that the masses and (vitally) their advisers failed to understand the nature of the astro-cycles and their transitory nature. As a result, they reacted blindly in predictable, automatic ways. Taking the impermanent to be permanent comes from not understanding the nature of change, and the fundamental financial fact — you cannot get something for nothing for ever. In all three downturns, the value of the astro-cycles is that understanding their specific meanings and knowing their timing offered advanced warning.

If we examine the deep symbolic meanings of contemporary astro-cycles, we will understand not only the path of delusion that brought us to the present crisis, but also what lies ahead. We may then be able to go one step further than our forebears — make far fewer mistakes in how we work our way of it. We may even turn disaster around and transform our world for the better.

Early reactions to the downturn have been impulsive, even chaotic — some policy-makers have behaved like headless chickens. People lauded as experts were mocked and cursed as exploiters or charlatans. Billions, even trillions, are being allocated to solutions that are unlikely to work. Like generals in a war, our politicians and economists seek to solve the problems of the future with weapons hardly suited to the past. How wasteful if they are wrong! How silly not to consider the insight astro-cycles might offer!

The next section will study in depth the path to our current crisis, hoping to put many of our false assumptions in perspective. The last section will then look at what lies ahead and see ways to make the very best use of the possibilities of the times.

1984-2008

Let's Party!

Chapter 4
Selling the Past

'What I ventured to question was the using of these huge sums as if they were income.' *Harold Macmillan* **explaining his criticism of Conservative privatisation**[14]

Most of the 53 'rock 'n roll' years leading up to 2008 could be seen as a constantly building party or celebration, interspersed with occasional periods of anxious 'going out for more supplies'.

The 1956-7 sign change of all planets from Jupiter outwards swept away what memories and values of the war years were left. With Neptune remaining in Scorpio until 1970 and Uranus building to conjunct Pluto in Virgo in 1965-6, past principles were challenged, found wanting and rejected, but not replaced. Pluto joining Uranus in Libra, and Neptune ingressing Sagittarius in 1970, heralded a decade that explored instability and unusual alternatives to a point of near anarchy. Instability and a chance to dream irresponsibly were the essence of the time. So, old battles were fought to the death without a thought for the consequences. The United Kingdom struggled over nationalisation, debt, workers' rights and the questioning of authority to the ultimate punk-rock level. The world saw conflicts and an ever-expanding arms race between the Soviet and Capitalist systems. The Middle East crisis expressed itself by war, terrorism and inflation in the price of oil. As misunderstanding proliferated, the world became increasingly dangerous. Racial and religious tension grew and the economic intervention of governments in the market place seemed to be increasingly counter-productive.

So, living through the nightmare of the last years of the Callaghan government in the UK and the first term of Margaret Thatcher until 1983, it may have seemed that the party was over. Far from it: really, it was yet to begin. This is where our story really starts.

The theory of marketplace 'discipline'

On 19 January 1984, Jupiter and Neptune entered Capricorn together, soon after Pluto had entered Scorpio to join Saturn. The astro background had shifted from over-reaching tolerance, belief in expansion and flexibility, to belief in intense realism based on what was measurable and practical. So the call went out — let the money and the financial markets decide. Free them from governmental political control to serve a particular party's interest group. Put away the idealist's unrealistic softness. Rely on collective common sense as epitomised by market forces. Good ideas will succeed and profit. Bad ideas will fail. Let the market decide winners and losers! All will learn from experience in the real world, not be protected from harsh realities. In such a competitive and innovative environment, fresh exciting enterprises will be launched and will flourish. The most brilliant and enterprising minds will rise naturally. Their success will trickle down to everyone. Our world will be vibrant, varied and exciting. All will benefit and be happy. At last we will be relieved from the incompetent rule of well intentioned, but misguided, zealots.

In the Saturn-dominated astrological circumstances of the time, to leave people unprotected to stand or fall and learn by facing the consequences of their desires seemed highly sensible. Because it took away the struggle for unrealistic theories and principles, it also seemed surprisingly liberating. Certainly it seemed to reflect the astro-cycles. With Pluto and Saturn in Scorpio and Neptune, triggered the first year by Jupiter in Capricorn, it seemed eminently appropriate and efficient for us to be responsible for ourselves and judged by the consequences. So it was, if you were willing to face those consequences. Not until 2008-9 were we to learn what this really meant and 'chicken out'. By then, it was rather late to change.

The practice of marketplace 'discipline'

The practice of a free-market based economy was full of paradox and contradiction. Although it sought to remove government intervention, trading rules, currency controls and restrictive working practices, the implications are essentially Saturnian. Because the economy was to be subject to the harsh practical reality of market forces, the weak and inefficient would be allowed to fail. Unemployment would be allowed to rise. Trade Union rights and welfare (started when Neptune was in the opposite sign of Cancer) were to be curtailed. Nationalised industries, the nations' assets (or 'Georgian silver' as the ex-Prime Minister Harold Macmillan referred to them), were to be sold to private investors and methods of competitive market efficiency created.

If harsh monetarist reality was good for the 'commanding heights of economy', it was also good for two other areas of assets, held in trust for ordinary people. These were the local authority-owned stock of rental property and the mutually owned building societies that financed much of the private mortgage market.

Like so many aspects of Thatcherite policies, the distribution of council houses to existing tenants at below market value prices seemed a success, and was a bonanza for some. A property-owning boom ensued. Similarly the deregulation of building societies gave a cash pay out or shareholding to all their member depositors. It created the 'healthy competition' of new players in the property market and banking industry. It released cash and assets for an increasing number of people. The appearance of short term prosperity stimulated a cash-rich boom into the late 1980s. Yet, and here comes the paradox, where is the control in all this? All we have really done is realise our assets and start to spend them. It was too early to assess the new policy. We were yet to experience the discipline of the free market.

Whether privatisation was right as a spur to greater operational efficiency or irresponsibly wrong in selling our key services to people interested only in profit became the main argument at the time. Similarly, the sale of council houses may have benefited sitting tenants, but was it at the expense of the housing needs of future generations? The de-regulation of building societies may have encouraged competition in the financial markets in the short term. However, by taking away protection, it opened the door to possible economic disaster. Northern Rock, Halifax, Bradford and Bingley, and others were to pay the price for their misused freedom in the 21st century loan market.

An even more important consideration was never properly considered — the misleading effect of releasing so much money into the hands of the government and speculators. The taste of wealth makes the appetite salivate for more. So, the search for speculative opportunities expanded into privately owed companies. Takeovers and asset stripping led to unemployment. Western financial institutions encouraged developing countries to balance their budgets and expand their economies by selling raw materials and cash crops. Social cohesion and who was profiting in those lands was hardly considered.

The West led the world into over-confidence at a time when the caution and good order of Saturn was essential to restructure our economies for future success. With so much to spend and credit available, asset values boomed. Britain and the world experienced an illusion of wealth. To have access to a percentage margin of this expanding illusion became 'economic reality'. No need to produce. The banks and booming service industries could bridge the gap. The rich nations needed to make less and less; just serve, spend and consume — enjoy!

The 'triumph' of capitalism
As the 1980s drew to a close and the leadership of Margaret Thatcher, Ronald Reagan and Michel Gorbachev was giving way to John Major, George H W Bush and Boris Yeltsin, Saturn and Uranus joined Neptune in Capricorn, to be opposed by Jupiter in Cancer. The fall of the Soviet Union, the descent of the Japanese Nikkei, the birth of modern China and the first Gulf War were accompanied by major correction and slow down in the great free-market experiment.

With all this came a major error — the assumption that capitalism had won its battle with Communism and Socialism. From this a number of non sequiturs were assumed to have followed. Capitalism was the best form of economic organisation and an ever-expanding free-market world economy was the way towards wealth and happiness for more and more people. Communism had failed. Not so. The Soviet Union was an incompetent form of clique-administered state capitalism. Modern China is a more successful example of this, which could conceivably materially surpass the Western democratic model. There is yet to be a truly Communist society anywhere in the world.

Whether capitalism had truly won or not, the damming defeat of its assumed opponents made it seem that way. So, the ideal of free-market economics sustained its standing through a difficult recession into 1993. Save for some anxious months following Saddam Hussein's 1990 invasion of Kuwait, the markets held up well through this time. They also made some difficult adjustments to accommodate and finance new nations from the old Soviet system. In September 1993, Jupiter in Libra completed its square to Uranus and Neptune. The next month, these were to make their final conjunction in Capricorn, whose ruler, Saturn, was pioneering a new trail in techno-keen Aquarius. This sign is to play a key role in our story through the chapters ahead.

The dangers of electronic free-trading markets

In 1986, the City of London had launched computer trading. After adjustments to it protect from mindless programme trading that had led to the 1987 crash; these developments introduced an entirely new generation of traders to the traditional City of London 'old pals' network. The new traders were short-term risk-takers. Their brilliant minds devised an ever-increasing range of derivatives, hedge trades and imaginative accounting that led to vast paper profits and bonuses to match.

Market forces allied with electronic accounting enabled numerous privatisations and takeovers. Ever-wider ranges of money-raising initiatives developed to enable mergers and the rewards of asset stripping. These and many other ways of creating immense short-term profits became the 'brilliant success story' of the City of London. We did not need an industrial base. We would produce the money and leave it to those in other countries to produce the goods at much lower prices, and profit from that as well.

Storing up problems for the future

Cash rich with new money, this constantly quick-changing trading environment led to fundamental errors in financial judgement that were destined to confuse monetarist-obsessed economists for a generation. The failure to understand the true meaning of what was happening from the early 1980s onward is a key root cause of our 21st century crisis. Even more worrying is that the errors generated by these times remain in the deluded assumptions and false thinking to be found in 2008-9 attempts to 'restore growth and prosperity'.

We did not understand then and are finding it difficult to understand today the harsh logic of Saturnian monetarism. If you wish to do as you like, you must be ready to accept and suffer the very worst consequences if you are wrong. If you wish to live by a market economy, it is illogical to 'stop the game', when the going gets too tough to contemplate. No institution is too important to fail. No consequence too dire to accept. That is market economics. It is logical and it works, but the endgame can be unbearably unpleasant.

Alternatively, you can get ahead of the market by limiting yourself to sensible behaviour. We could have transferred and reinvested private and previous publicly-owned assets for everyone's long-term benefit. Instead, we squandered them on a bean feast. We believed indiscriminate consumption would make us rich for ever — the link between spending and earning would never end. We partied on extravagant champagne

Using an understanding of the intrinsic nature of Saturn and Capricorn would have led to more cautious examination of what was happening. We would have seen the very short-term nature of the speculative bubble. We would have asked what happens when there are no more assets to sell and house prices reach their optimum level.

In Chapters 7 and 8, we will see what happens when the proceeds of the sale of assets, whether publicly or privately owned, are spent. We will see into what strange waters de-regulation led financial institutions. The consequences of economies becoming over-dependent on the service sector and consumption to take up the slack will be revealed.

However, right now we are only in 1994 and the party is far from over. The 'fun' is only just beginning. Read on to learn of the ingenious way we kept it going, even when there were few assets left to sell.

Chapter 5
Recession and Recovery — Really?

The deficit created by Ronald Reagan and George H W Bush, to be inherited by the next President, was so central to the 1992 election that a third candidate, Ross Perot, gained considerable support by making it the campaign issue. In the United Kingdom, speculation against the British pound had thrown Britain out of the European Exchange Rate Mechanism. The slow down in economic activity reached a nadir in the early autumn of 1992. This is how it miraculously recovered!

From bust to boom
From 1992 until 1993 sentiment felt fragile. After rising strongly in 1993, markets corrected downward until the end of 1994. Then an exponential rise in equities occurred. It was unlike any seen before. From just under 3100 points at the beginning of 1995, the FTSE more than doubled to 6950 on the last day of 1999. In the same period, the DJIA rose from 3700 to 11,750.

This boom was to allow the Clinton two-term Presidency to end in 2000 with the US having transformed a deep deficit into a healthy surplus. Behind it lay the 'miracle' workings of Alan Greenspan, the head of the US Federal Reserve. Changes in interest rates and money supply skilfully manipulated expectation. Electronic trading systems allowed more and more new players and their money into the markets. One of the first acts of the new UK Labour government in 1997 was to give the Bank of England the power to decide interest rates. At the same time, the government removed the teeth of its responsibility, by giving most of its regulatory powers to a new insider-run Financial Services Agency. All these combined to self-fulfil expectation.

In addition to this money manipulation, as the 20th century came to an end there was all that new digital technology to invest in. Whether it was internet stocks, entertainment media, mobile phone, surveillance and other communications technology, we entered the 21st century with the prospect before us of unlimited growth and prosperity for all.

The astro-cycles explain it

To what extent do the astro-cycles explain, confirm or caution the optimism with which we moved through the 1990s and entered the new millennium?

The 1993 US Presidential Inauguration Chart [15] indicated very different outcomes to those the campaign had led the people to expect. With Mercury hardly aspected in Capricorn culminating and the Moon, also in Capricorn, opposing Mars in Cancer, which was applying to oppose Uranus/Neptune, many Clinton election promises were not fulfilled. Through the first two years markets rose and then corrected back down again. However, in late 1994 until early 1995, Jupiter and Pluto entered Sagittarius and Mars made its biennial retrogression — this time in Leo. The Sagittarius/Leo astro-cycles indicated a speculative surge — death and transformation through expansion.

As well as the Pluto-in-Sagittarius-driven mass taste for expansion just for the sake of it, the astro-cycles seemed to offer another very rational justification. In April 1995 Uranus entered Aquarius, to be joined there in 1998 by Neptune. Both ingresses symbolised a taste for heightened technological innovation that continues until the mutual reception completes with Uranus leaving Pisces and Neptune leaving Aquarius in 2010-11. For 15 years, new technology, discovery, expertise, economic innovation and visions of global revolution that will 'benefit everyone without end' have driven the economic agenda. Nothing has been impossible. The combination of new knowledge and methods, with Pluto in expansive Sagittarian flexibility, was so powerful that only the most 'old-fashioned' and 'kill-joy' 'dinosaurs' would dare to question what was happening. Growth was king; growth without end!

Well, not quite! In early May 2000, a stellium built in Taurus. It consisted of the Sun and Moon, plus the five inner planets in a square to Aquarian Uranus and Neptune. Then in September 2001, Saturn opposed Pluto on the USA chart's [16] Ascendant/Descendant axis signalling a dramatic confrontation with reality. Equities struggled and failed to recover back to the highs of the spring of 2000. Two critical oppositions brought negative news (Saturn in Gemini opposed Pluto in Sagittarius 2001-2) and deluded expectations (Jupiter in Leo opposed Neptune in Aquarius 2002-3). While these two remained in orb, we saw the DJIA double bottom below 7500 in October 2002 and March 2003.

This was to be no more than a two to three year decline. Reducing interest rates and a very relaxed lending regime led to a booming property market and hence ever more collateral to support debt. Once the oppositions were out of orb, with plenty of Aquarian and Sagittarian drive remaining, the world economy was to experience an exhilarating recovery to even greater heights. The Sagittarian Pluto and the ingenious Piscean/Aquarian mutual reception between Uranus and Neptune fuelled tax and interest rate cuts that artificially expanded demand. This increased production and hence equity values. Yet, with Chinese and Indian low-wage labour forces becoming engaged, prices remained stable. The value of our assets rose to greater heights than the 1990s. So, we could borrow and spend more and more. Pluto was in Sagittarius ruled by Jupiter. Yes sure, let us expand to death!

Ignoring the astro cycles exposed us to danger

Wise astrologers were not convinced. As well as the ever-present danger of taking on too much when Sagittarius is around, the clue lay in an unbelievable house price boom occurring while Saturn was transiting Cancer, the sign that symbolises the home. Saturn suggests structure and realism. Were we heading for a downturn again as in the late 1980s, or could we really have become so innovative and brilliant that the old rules no longer applied? Looking back from what we now know, it is clear that we were just delaying the inevitable. Incredibly ingenious hedging and new instruments to buy and sell debt, based upon inaccurate assessments of income status and risk, were fuelling an unsustainable boom.

If economic planners then had used astro-cycles as a tool of assessment, they would have seen the danger and taken action to avert it. Seeing how people and society were ignoring the need to reassess while Saturn was transiting Cancer (= limitation in the home) and Leo (= limitation through speculation) clearly indicated the dangers of their actions. This is the proper way to assess whether an economy is well or badly set for the future. If we go out naked on a frosty day we may save a little time. However, by not bothering to dress up warm, our body strength will soon expire and leave us behind those who took longer to prepare.

As we shall see in the next chapter, there were other ways that astro-cycles were ignored and so the UK and world economy accelerated along the road to ruin.

Chapter 6
No More Past to Sell — Let's Sell the Future

'As Pluto establishes itself in Capricorn, the other outer planets change sign and we build toward the 2010-11 major cardinal T-square between Pluto in Capricorn, Jupiter/Uranus in Aries and Saturn in Libra, something ... real and effective ... will need to be done. This will not just be with regard to ecology. Whether the current world economy is sustainable as it is will also be questioned. With fire, air and mutability dominant for so long, we have become convinced we can 'get away with it' for ever.' **(Published one month before DJIA reached its all-time-high of 14,198 in October 2007, written in July for an early August deadline): 'Working with the Planets'** *The Astrological Journal* **(Sept 2007).**

Chapter 4 described the sale of assets accrued in the past to release capital, while subjecting traditional industries to the harsh reality of market forces. The misuse of the consequently acquired assets and efficiency savings squandered the opportunity for sustainable economic restructuring that Saturn, Uranus and Neptune in Capricorn offered. Judgements were based on ever shorter-term profit considerations. We ignored any other consequences. The experts who guided our lives in these new and 'enlightened' financial times somehow did not notice or talk about the 'elephant in the medium to long term market forces room'!

Let us say again that accepting the market knows best is intrinsically valid, provided you are willing to allow enterprises to face the consequences unflinchingly. The outcome of a bad decision must run its course, no matter how much suffering results. No matter if all banks fail, millions starve, the planetary eco-system is destroyed. In the end, what is dysfunctional will collapse — only the strong will survive. This is the logic of a genuine free-enterprise market economic model.

The problem with such a strategy is that the price to be paid for failure can be so dire that no one is willing to pay it. Instead we employ the best minds to find ways to avoid reality — the Greenspan solution examined in Chapter 5. This not only puts off the inevitable, but also makes it worse. So strategies become more obscure and arcane, while all the time making worse the ultimate unbearable consequences.

Sustaining monetarism without money

We have seen that monetarism seemed to work well for most people, while there was lots of money from sold assets around. It continued to seem efficient as more and more companies were taken over and asset stripped to the benefit of the new owners. Teams of accountants scrutinised balance sheets and cut out hidden perks to the public and staff. Call centres with endless voice menus were opened and then outsourced to Asia. Targets for employees and the public were set. We celebrated our efficiency, whatever the price in irritation and lowering motivation.

However, as the 20th century gave way to the 21st and the takeover boom slackened, more creative ways to sustain an expanding economy were devised. Typically low-level Aquarian in their well-intentioned but misplaced brilliance, and typically low-level Sagittarian in their over-accepting lack of structure, the short-term nature of these ways became ever more dangerous.

The United Kingdom government found ingenious ways to spend off the balance sheet. It financed Higher Education through student loans and organised the capital building of schools, hospital and transport renewal through public finance initiatives. Such a live now/pay later hire purchase created a very real debt burden for decades ahead. How unwise to increase unsupported debt, rather than save, at a time of booming consumption, low inflation and high government income!

In 18 years British Conservative governments had sold the past. Now Labour governments over 11 prosperous years had sold our future — even the nation's gold assets in a bear market at a quarter of their 2008 value.

The behaviour of private financiers was even more surreal. To keep the bonuses coming in, artificial values were assumed and traded. Debt was bought, sold and competitively sought after. The financial world seemed to be following the gospel according to Robert Maxwell — manipulating prices higher and ignoring intrinsic value. Debt was so prized and appeared so profitable to financial traders that the public were encouraged to borrow more and more. Interest-free transfer holidays between credit cards became a standard strategy. The expansion of property price values extended to ever more distant parts of the world, as it became ever easier to borrow on one property to finance another. Misleading debt-default estimates kept illusory assets moving between institutions. All was new 'profitable' business, to count for the annual bonus. Most ordinary people gaped and accepted in wonder. It seemed too good to be true, but our brilliant bankers and economists were much wiser than us. 'We are living in enlightened times, in an ever-expanding world economy from which all could benefit.'

Astro-cycles of reality
Not for much longer, though! The astro-cycles were indicating that the day of reckoning was at hand. As in 1720, it was a Saturn/Neptune opposition just past the middle of fixed signs that headed a climax of speculative delusion. Neptune, unless inspired by selfless giving to others, leads to self-deception. The opposition by Saturn therefore suggests a time when deceptive structures are bound to fail, even though they will be desperately persisted with until the opposition is complete. In early August 1720 the opposition was within a 4 degree orb. In 2007, sub-prime uncertainties first emerged in August when Saturn was moving on 4 degrees from the completed opposition.

At the time most people felt this was no more than a temporary blip. A strategy of tax cuts and reduced interest rates would encourage spending again, as it had in the 1990s and 2003. Such attempts to sustain the market managed to hold up prices until the 14 October top.

However, now it was to be very different. As well as the end of the clouding delusion of the Saturn/Neptune opposition, far more radical changes were on their way. As the early sub-prime mortgage warnings intensified, on 24 November 2007 Uranus was to make a direct station just a few minutes of arc away from its position at the peak of the German hyperinflation in 1923. Perhaps 84 years later only Zimbabwe was deluded enough to actually print money in a futile attempt to escape a crisis. Yet in essence, how different from printing money was the irresponsible encouragement of debt? Indeed we shall see in the next chapter that, as other stimulus strategies failed to work in 2009, reserve banks were to resort to 'quantitative easing' (i.e. printing money)!

Other than those who had full access to and understanding of the banks' corporate balance sheets, astrologers were the first to feel uneasy. They knew Pluto was edging toward Capricorn and from the end of 2008 Saturn commenced a five-fold opposition to Uranus that would not complete until 2010. Even the downgrading of Pluto to a dwarf planet in 2006 could not cloud their eyes from the harsh dose of reality that lay ahead.

The boom times were coming to an end. The wise were beginning to see that all methods of short-term artificial economic stimulus were exhausted. Very soon there would be nowhere to run.

2008-2010

Party Over!

Chapter 7
The Danger of Denial

'Indeed, it could be argued that for the 21 years or more since the London Big Bang introduction of electronic trading, it is the new money and new derivative instruments that have kept the financial markets not just afloat, but expanding rapidly.

'Big question, can this introduction of new money or ways of hedging and offsetting continue indefinitely? Big problem, Pluto is leaving Sagittarius and, through 2008, establishing itself with Jupiter in Capricorn. The over-optimism that has encouraged us to use our Aquarian technological brilliance to find ways to expand, consume and speculate to death is in its very end days. Quite simply, we cannot go on as we are. The financial ingenuity will have to give way to realism – especially with Saturn now in Virgo.' **(DJIA was at 12,576 when published and due to rise to 13,132 in May 2008, written mid-January 2008 for a February deadline): 'Working with the Planets'** *The Astrological Journal* **(March 2008).**

The enormity of what was happening — essentially the near bankruptcy of a large proportion of the world banking industry, the consequent lack of credit, downturn of demand and unemployment — was too much to understand, let alone accept at first. As time goes by, the public has become accustomed to expressing contempt for leading bankers, 'qualified' financial advisers and the politicians who were pleased to ride on their coat tails. They are forgetting the untouchable awe in which they had held them until 2008. How could it be that these experts did not know what they were permitting and advising, had failed to weigh the consequences and did not know the answers?

Denial[17]
In 2007, the first stories of sub-prime mortgages, credit defaults swaps and banks being exposed to liabilities of billions, if not trillions, of dollars all seemed very distant and arcane. Most people ignored the warning signs of

Pluto's temporary ingress into Capricorn between late January and mid-June 2008. They were sufficiently reassured by its return to Sagittarius and happy to focus on the greatest Olympic extravaganza of all time. Opening with traditional Chinese auspiciousness at 8 p.m. on the 8th day of the 8th month of 2008 certainly symbolised a great organisational achievement. However, Western numerologists noting eight to be the number of Saturn wondered how much there was to celebrate, when so many problems were being covered up, both inside and outside the Chinese nation.

In the weeks that followed, it became clear that the Olympics had been the world's final spree and throw of caution to the wind. Understanding the astrology would have made this obvious well in advance. For, on 9 September 2008, with the games hardly over, Pluto moved into direct motion and edged uncompromisingly towards Capricorn. Also approaching was another dramatic anniversary for the UK economy.

The iconic 1978-9 Winter of Discontent crossroads in Britain's industrial relations intensified to a climax on 22 January 1979. By 21 February most workers had accepted substantial wage increases and started to return to work. Through these weeks Saturn retrograded between 12 and 11 degrees Virgo. The exact Saturn return for 22 January 1979 occurred on 14 Sept 2008. At that time Saturn was moving forwards quickly to oppose Uranus on 4 November. On the last day of 2008, it slowed to a retrograde station. On 17 May 2009 it made a direct station at 14Vi54. It is no coincidence that the Saturn return of that 1979 moment, so important in the world accepting monetarist free-market economics, should signal a massive global downturn as a direct consequence of the failure of those monetarist policies.

Anger and bargaining and yet more denial
So it was that the Olympic athletes and public were hardly settled back into normality when, towards the end of the month, a terrible lingering truth became a known public reality. Enormous sums of money had been lost,

even more were needed if the bank deposit savings of millions of people were not to be wiped out. With Saturn in Virgo applying to oppose Uranus in Pisces, ever-diversifying harsh realities were piling up, one dire fact of financial disaster after another. Our faith in the great institutions we had considered to form the very bedrock of financial probity was shattered. Experts queued on the news channels to admit what they had learned or even taught at business school had not covered this. In short, they did not know what to do next!

Before Pluto made its main ingress into Capricorn on 27 November 2008, a mania of revelations was driven by the first in that series of five Saturn/Uranus oppositions, due to be exact on the day of the US Presidential election — 4 November 2008.

With Pluto still in Sagittarius, our leaders behaved like orphans in the storm, buffeted by forces they did not understand and could not control. As massive guarantees were not sufficient and quick-fix interest rate reductions became meaningless, they ran around like headless chickens. Amidst the anger, denial persisted and politicians insisted that this downturn in the cycle would soon pass. They would help us through it, and trading and prosperity would then 'return to normal'.

Before it happened the media had been so intimidated by the affluent splendour of the 'captains of finance' that they too had been seduced by mantras of economic miracle. So, even when they saw the 'writing on the wall' and faced the stark reality, the media continued to see as 'experts' the very economists who had presided over the actions that created the crisis.

Because these same deluded 'economic experts' remained in charge, deep in the rationale of their actions to meet the crisis remained an unwavering deluded denial. In spite of everything, it was only a matter of time before the markets recovered and we could return to the good times of 2007. So government bank bail outs were chosen as the best method. Bank debt and exposure to liability were exchanged for share equity.

'Once the economy and share values recovered, the peoples' investment could be sold back to private investors. Then all would be well again,' they explained. 'We may even make a profit!'

Problem: what would happen if the government had to meet their liability for all the hundreds of billions of exposure and the bank share price did not recover, because there were no private investors to buy bank shares?

Hoping to avert this possibility and help everyone through these bad times, stimulus packages were devised in many G20 countries. Many were a hotchpotch of wishful thinking and plans for capital developments that should have been funded by the Reagan/Thatcher boom in the 1980s, or the booms during the late 1990s and early 21st century. China made the most radical change of all. Its buying of Western debt had been a key factor in enabling the consumer boom. The abrupt halt of this boom in 2008 now threatened Chinese social stability, as its rapid-growth, export-based economy declined. To answer the pressures of unemployment, Chinese people were encouraged to change their traditional habits and spend like the West[18]. The Chinese government aimed to move the foundation of its economy from exports to home consumption. It sought to achieve this by a US$595 billion government fiscal stimulus and the building of new rail links, financed by favourable bank loans. It also aimed to avoid layoffs, late wage payments and cuts. Slogans such as 'Dare to spend', as a patriotic act were displayed. Bearing in mind the very strong July 2009 Solar Eclipse's path exactly over the Chinese commercial Shanghai heartland[19], it could be argued that such a desperate strategy indicates not so much an economic solution as a final emptying of the world's monetary kitty.

Such acceptance of massive debt to support 'toxic loan' exposure or finance stimulus packages is a vain attempt to restore 2007-level prosperity. This yearning to bargain for a quick return to an expanding world economy reveals a deeply dangerous sense of intransigent denial — an unwillingness to learn.

The policy makers of 2008-9 did not understand that what had appeared to work so well for the last 15 years had been sustained by false accounting and deception. The Dow reached above 14,000, because credit was out of control and world financial recording deceptively obscured the reasons. Now, all was bust; attempting to return to the recent past was unbelievably counterproductive, because it was a retreat from reality. Pluto was in Capricorn. The Aquarian focus was fading and technological innovation would soon be scaled down from new products to consolidation.

In their desperation these crisis-creating leaders initiated one half-considered initiative after another. Like over-protective, guilt-ridden parents, desperately fearing they are failing their children, they acted with undue haste. They were too full of anxiety to dare to give any of their initiatives a chance to bear fruit.

Acceptance

The chapters that follow will explain a wide range of astro-cycles that suggest we are at a radical turning point. We need to step back, think more and do less for a while. We need to weigh and compare financial with other world social problems and find ways of making one problem answer another. Difficult times may lead to desperate experiences, but that does not mean that desperate speed in our actions will produce the correct solutions. The astro-cycles suggest we need leaders who realise this and that it could take some years to correct the consequences of their predecessors' initial hastiness.

Chapter 8
Understanding Sustainable Growth

'Problems cannot be solved with the
same consciousness that created them.'
Albert Einstein

The early months of World War Two were referred to as the 'phoney war'. Britain had declared war upon the best armed and most brutal dictator of all time, but life continued very much as before. It seemed rather like this for much of 2009. The figures and projections for the future suggested dire doom, out of which no one could see a way. Yet, life was not that bad! Unemployment and debt exposure were growing for more and more people, but the majority continued to enjoy the temporary respite provided by numerous frantic government attempts to save the day. They heard talk of massive debt burdens, expenditure cuts and tax increases to come, but were so far cushioned from the worst effects of the downturn. Saturn may be opposed to Uranus, but the planets were in mutable signs. The mass consciousness was not ready to accept the worst. Surely we would find a way around it!

A 15 year period of change
Certainly that was the mood at the April 2009 G20 meeting in London of the leaders controlling 85 per cent of the world economy. With the Moon in Cancer trined with Mars in Pisces, the meeting offered sympathetic cooperation[20]. Yet, the Moon also squared the Sun, Venus and Mercury in Aries and Venus squared Pluto. So, a struggle to find any fundamental and effective agreement was anticipated. With Saturn retrograding in Virgo opposed by Mars in Pisces across the 10th/4th houses, even a walk out was mentioned. Fortunately, Mars built to conjunct Gordon Brown's Jupiter[21] early on 4 April. To crown it, the Sun on the day was 12 Aries in a trine to 12 Leo where the Brown natal Moon meets the Obama Sun[22]. The two men just could not stop beaming at each other

and express a radiance that spread to the other world leaders.

Of course, the Aries planets said it all. It was too early to be clear. The bonding and commitment towards working together was certainly most valuable, but were the proposals more than stop-gap credit arrangements and decisions on new regulations that will, in turn, be 'got around'? It was rather like looking for a new romantic relationship too soon after the painful ending of the one before. Too much yearning for and seeking what has been lost leads to the danger of making the same mistakes again. Helping ordinary people through their immediate economic pain may be necessary, but to expect to bounce the world economy back to 'health' is a major delusion. A radical realignment of the world economy lies ahead. This Aries meeting can be seen as no more than kick-starting a 15-year process of fundamental economic realignment.

This time we must learn from past errors

At an earlier meeting on 31 January 2009, just six days before the second Saturn/Uranus opposition; Gordon Brown had addressed his co-creators of the world economic crisis at the World Economic Forum in Switzerland. He told them that there was no previous historical experience of what was happening. Essentially, they had to learn what to do next from what happened next! The astrology both questions and confirms his words.

He is wrong because in the past, as now, we have always had the astro-cycles to help us see through the nature of mass delusion, but have chosen to ignore them. Elements in the South Sea Bubble, 1835-42 and 1929-33 Depressions and their aftermaths offer many lessons we can draw on. To start with, these experiences show the futility of the early talk of 'weathering a downturn in the economic cycle' and attempts to manipulate early recovery. Certainly, it is not the first time that we have faced a stage in the *cosmic* cycle that exposes our hubris and over-reaching arrogance. Belief in endless growth and something-for-nothing characterised all three previous boom and bust periods studied in Chapter 3. Until we use astro-cycles as early warnings in our culture, the same mistakes will be made by future generations.

Ecological threat offers economic solution

Yet Gordon Brown is right in that this is the first time, due to our industrial mechanical science-driven economy, that the deception of endless growth has been extended so globally. Pluto has returned to Capricorn (symbolises death and regeneration of business structures) for the first time since 1762-77 — the beginning of the Industrial Revolution. For a decade and a half ahead, we face a radical reassessment of our achievements over the past 250 years.

Nor is it an unconnected coincidence that this happens in the midst of threatened global ecological disaster. Our inventive arrogance led us to assume we can change the earth — even explain and re-invent every aspect of life itself. We have boasted of defeating limitation. Did we really think we could force Saturn to serve our childish experiments? We have tried the patience of the natural order. While Pluto transits Saturn's sign, we have to learn the true nature of structure and responsibility.

The changes are even more radical than this. This Pluto return is similar to the one before the last that occurred in the early 16th century. During the 80 years before that all the outer-planets followed very similar paths in the zodiac to those 80 years before the present time. In the 15th/16th centuries, the development of printing and the translation of texts into the vernacular gave many new people access to knowledge. An educated public began to question the abuse of trust of those in power. The Pluto Capricorn transit (1515-32) saw challenges to the papacy and the emergence of Lutheran and Anglican Protestantism In the 20th/21st centuries, the internet is having a similar effect. In May 2009 British politicians faced unprecedented exposure and condemnation over their expense claims.

The questioning will move even further. The earlier time was, of course, the very seed point of modern science. Today, we face a radical reassessment of the nature of that science and its role in society's decision-making processes. Hopefully, this time we will not see centuries of conflict and repression, but the old and new will welcome each other in, cross-fertilise and restore balance and success

Abandoning the simplistic notions of growth
Pluto and Saturn dominating and correcting Jupiter-like excess will make it clear why we need to reject the notion of growth as the measure of success and failure, happiness and unhappiness. It will be difficult for economists and politicians to do so. After victory in World War II, expansion, consumption and especially 'growth' replaced 'victory' as the elixir of happiness offered by all who sought success in public life. On offer was 'growth', where everyone could have what they wanted at the expense of no one else — even the richest person in the world would not have to pay. In time, 'growth' would make everyone happy — even the poorest African peasant. Brilliant economic minds and business theorists devised complex financial systems to manipulate the balance sheets and hide the real price each person was paying. Buying now and paying later offered early enjoyment. Exploitation and its consequences were too distant in place and time to be of concern. Enjoying the fruits of luxury, but not yet having to pay, was seductive. It was only a matter of time and education, it seemed, before everyone who accepted democracy and global free-market capitalism would be well fed and would live in peace.

Pluto's ingress into Capricorn comes after a period, from 2001, when the sign's ruler Saturn opposed Pluto, Neptune and then Uranus. Now the price of ignoring these warnings cannot be avoided. Finally we face down the nonsensical inadequacy of 'endless growth' as a solution to anything. The longer our economic 'experts' and the politicians that listen to them focus strategies upon this lost cause, the more pain and disappointment they and we will experience in the end. In this sense, Gordon Brown is truly right. It is new. Technology is so powerful and the world is so interconnected that growth as he understands it can no longer be sustained.

Why we need to search for sustainable growth

Now, this is not bad news. Saturn is our greatest friend who only denies us what would not work, but instead bring pain. Properly understood and utilised, Saturn only insists upon limiting what is destined to bring disappointment and failure. Overindulgence leads to nausea, bad health and early death. This should not surprise us. The essential principle of modern mechanical science is that, while you can use energy more efficiently, there is never anything for nothing. Each side of every equation must balance. Energy may transform the nature of a mass. Combining particular masses may create energy, but all is transformed in a balanced way. There is never something for nothing. Claims that 'magic' is possible are the very things that annoy material scientists the most. So how can economists who suggest that endless growth is scientific be taken seriously?

Saturn is the friend of modern science and anyone seriously wishing to find a lasting economic answer. Saturn does not deny growth, only unsustainable growth. We need to be scientific is the deepest sense. Not just see the pursuit of science as obtaining research funding that benefits the provider, at the cost of the environment. Science should be used to balance the books of our relationship with the planet and each other.

A sustainable economic recovery will require us to borrow to invest, but only in a sustainable future. It will make immense work demands upon millions of people. Some will find survival difficult; many will have to accept less. As in wartime, all these limitations will be bearable, even welcomed, if we can see a more efficient and sustainable future being the product of our endeavours. Would not most of us prefer this? Do we really want to be given borrowed money, to spend on what we do not need in the vain hope the world will forget 2008/2010 and a new prosperity will 'magically' arise?

For, as we have seen in earlier chapters, the kind of bubble that burst in 2008 is only ever sustainable for a temporary period, which lasts as long as a suitably misunderstood astro-cycle lasts. This misunderstanding always leads to future disaster.

In contrast, the development of a sustainable world economy is a step-by-step learning process – ideally suited for this 15-year period with Pluto in Capricorn. In early 2009, there are few signs that any world leader or economist realises this. They, as we, will have to learn by the experience of our failures and successes. Using debt to develop work and enterprise that builds infrastructure and sustainable energy generation may be a start, but it goes much deeper. It is necessary to identify the core values behind what we want and why.

The core values of sustainable growth

Harmony and happiness may seem curious words to use in a discussion on economic theory. They are, however, the essential touchstone to determine what will and will not work in restructuring and hence rebuilding our world economy on sustainable principles. So, the lasting benefit for all is the touchstone to finding a way out of our current crisis. It involves seeking happiness for as many creatures as a possible, to harm as few as possible, to wish and act so that all can be happy. Hardship becomes easier to bear when challenges bring out the best behaviour in all people. In difficult, Saturn-dominated times there will be temptations that punish and bring pain if we fall into them. When we do not close the arms factory making cluster bombs because people need work, thousands of innocents lose limbs and everyone loses the right to be happy. When we close our eyes to human rights abuses, lest business deals be lost; buy sweat-shop-made clothes or consume we do not need; burn fuel unnecessarily; pollute and cause illness; indulge in extravagance with money manipulated from the disadvantaged; keep the truth from the public to profit and gain power; manipulate balance sheets; spin lies and false promises; abuse our privilege; work too hard and ignore our children; and act in any way that harms others, we play our part in the creation of an unhappy and unsustainable world. All such actions combine and distort our minds to bad judgements that in turn will come back to destroy the lives of ourselves, our families, friends and nations.

What actions bring sustainable growth?

As we examine every decision and initiative in our individual and collective lives, both politicians and media should stop pretending they know what should be done, or even that they know who might know. Now is a time of humility to learn from events. Chapter 4 showed that capitalism did not win in 1989. The Soviet system failed. Indeed, the world economy is beyond a battle for the principles of capitalism, growth and free trade against state control. We are suffering the consequences of the failure of all of them and their lack of honesty. We suffer from the many methods of manipulating money by balance sheets. Our society has been broken by the mental confusion and distortion engendered in each individual mind by commercial media and advertising. The false and unholy hopes so sown could in the end prove to be as bad for us as rule by a centralised politburo. The world economy can only be viable if it is based upon the common sense fundamental financial fact outlined in the first chapter.

Confronting reality may at first seem disappointing. Then we see it really helps to know there are no miracle-working experts. There never were. We need to work out actions and methods together and explain the possibilities and uncertainties honestly to each other. Free enterprise works to the extent that it recognises that ordinary people on the ground are wiser. The strength of an unregulated economy is the refreshing common sense of those at the cutting edge. The unfortunate weakness of free enterprise is that such common sense is too easily drowned out by media and marketing manipulation, seeking to serve a few greedy people.

So, every suggested solution must be put to the test of fundamental cost effectiveness. Is what it gives and takes balanced? Will this action degenerate and exploit or regenerate and heal? Will outcomes leave people feeling disappointed and cheated, or experiencing the kindness of a pleasant surprise? Does what we promote promise far more than it delivers, or inspire gratitude and generosity in our hearts by delivering more than expected? That we must consider ways of achieving such ideals is good news. It will help us to learn lessons and avoid the negative consequences of self-delusion.

Using astro-cycles to assess sustainability

With Saturn in mutable Virgo opposed Uranus in mutable Pisces, 2008-10, we will see many attempts being made to avoid or divert consequences and deny what the planets suggest is coming. Billions are being borrowed, spent and/or risked by governments. Quantitative easing increases the money supply. All could dissolve into mutable nothingness and make the long term worse. Pluto is in Saturn's earthy sign. The cosmic response will be uncompromising. 'Get it right or suffer!' Seeking to avoid will only make things worse.

In addition to the 15 years in which Pluto symbolizes the need to face the truth or continue to suffer the consequences; the five Saturn/Uranus oppositions do not bode well for technology. The first four (4 November 2008, 5 February, 15 September 2009 and 26 April 2010) are across the mutable Virgo/Pisces axis. After the 26 July 2010 completion in cardinal signs, Jupiter and Uranus both drift back to Pisces until January/March 2011. This prelude to Neptune leaving Aquarius and entering Pisces in April 2011 could diminish the taste for invention and technology. Cost savings could lead to system breakdowns caused by poor maintenance and planning. Too many satellites orbiting the planet and too little regulation, poor private control, the impoverishment of the old Soviet programme; all could lead to collisions, pollution of space and communication breakdowns on Earth itself.

Two to three days before the second Saturn-in-Virgo/Uranus-in-Pisces opposition on 5 February 2009, two sonar 'cloaked' nuclear submarines collided in the Atlantic Ocean, but did not realise they had done so until returning to port! A week later, on 12 February 2009, two light training planes crashed, tragically killing two young cadets on their first flight. The same day mobile satellite phone service provider Iridium had one of its orbiting satellites knocked offline when it collided with a non-working Russian satellite. This created a band of dust around the planet. On 12 February, there was a T-square between Moon in Libra, Venus in Aries and Pluto in Capricorn; very close to the degrees of the July 2010 Jupiter/Uranus, Saturn/Mars and Pluto T-square.

As economic circumstances deteriorate, the resources needed to take action will be difficult to find. When Aquarius was dominant and confident, it was easy to blast objects into space. Navigation devices seemed to offer limitless communication facilities. Then Pluto was in Sagittarius. With that planet now in the next sign, manufacturing has slowed dramatically. Currency level changes can radically affect imports and exports. As communication breaks down, dependence upon technology will become less certain and satisfying.

More dominant will be sympathy and sacrifice, as we struggle desperately to have some realistic and effective impact on our circumstances. Policy-makers will be full of words saying what should be done, but reluctant to accept just how radical a change is needed; not only in method, but in who knows the answers.

The astro-cycles confirm that the solution does not lie in growth for its own sake. Returning to busy energy-intensive hyperactivity would be pointless. Encouraging impulsive spending will not regenerate the economy. The benefits will fail to materialise, while debt becomes astronomical. Instead we should honour the natures of Saturn and Pluto. If we do so, we will find relief from anxiety and suffering and happy outcomes. Saturn brings realism to situations. Pluto undermines in order to regenerate. Once we accept the need for this realism and radical change, we are on the path to recovery. Here is how it works.

Economic solution that leads to better lives

Weigh each activity and investment for its effect and effectiveness. Why do our society and media spend large sums of money to persuade us to work long hours to earn sufficient to buy what we do *not* need? Can we survive by sharing resources and consuming less? How many journeys do we need to make? The ecological debate is the opposite of what has been assumed. Rather than asking whether in times of economic downturn we can afford to care for the environment, we should realise that meeting environmental demands answers the needs of the economy. Have at least one genuine day of rest each week — maybe more. We can downsize, consume less, maintain and repair more and focus on quality of life. Every aspect of our individual and social lives can be reassessed for their usefulness. Find ways of saving money and consumption, sharing and supporting each other. Not the 'curse' of unemployment, but the blessing of less work, more play, more friends. This not only matches, but answers both the economic and ecological needs. 'Spend and work economically — result happiness. Spend to maximise profit and work excessively — result misery' could be the Micawberesque dictum for the 21st century. When this is realised, Saturn and Pluto become our greatest friends.

It will be a difficult pill to swallow for 'yesterday's' economists. Many clever marketing minds will need to develop their ethical side before coming on board. Yet only when those who make policy see this truth will we be in tune with the astro-cycles of the times. However difficult the transits may be, as soon as one person, a group, a whole society or world does that, they will feel much happier. Then life becomes far easier for everyone.

When we see this and our strategies become wiser, we will have suffered just enough to accept radical change in our assumptions about growth and to know the true priorities of the 21st century global economy.

And all this is just the beginning

Yet, as we shall see in the concluding chapters, to think like this in 2010 will be very early days. Neptune and Chiron have to establish themselves in Pisces, as well as Jupiter and Uranus back in Aries, before we will even get started.

There is no guarantee that the path of common sense will be followed. Nations may take more narrow and aggressive views. People may be unable to see beyond blame and the need to struggle, even fight, for the limited resources available. Pity when it turns to self-pity can be a lethal force that justifies the greatest persecutions and injustices. A dysfunctional world of peoples who blame each other can soon turn the opportunity of loving understanding to the curse of ignorant hate. World War II started after a ten year struggle to recover from the 1929 Wall Street Crash.

The positive good sense this chapter is floundering towards will be very new and may seem naïve, but it will work when economists and ecologists see that they are facing the same crisis. They hold in their hands the solution to each other's problems. The cares of global and anti-global campaigners coincide. When scientists broaden what they will accept as science, they will strengthen, not undermine, their effectiveness. Scientific innovation with astro-cycle insight means effective objectivity. From this comes sustainable right outcomes at right times.

The chapters that follow weigh these positive and negative possibilities.

2010-24

Lasting Economic Solutions?

Outer Planets 2010-24

Jupiter changes sign every year and completes 1.25 cycles in the period. Saturn changes every 2 to 3 years as indicated

Explanation The above diagram shows the outer planetary movements for 2010-24. The lines from Pluto, Neptune and Uranus represent their slow progress. Saturn and Jupiter move faster. By considering the combined effect of all the planetary positions, the chapters that follow assess how we may experience particular years or sub-periods. Underlying the whole period will be the Pluto-in-Capricorn transformation.

Chapter 9
2010-12 — Understanding the Transition

'The three main reasons for the fall of the Roman Empire
were self-interest, hidden hatreds and "youthful[23]" counsel.'
Displayed by *Elizabeth I* as a salutary warning

The economic world picture that develops through 2010-12 will be very different to that pictured in the minds of economists who used their old tools to forecast recovery commencing in 2010. The experience of economic uncertainty will have and will continue to change old attitudes, tastes and loyalties. Recovery, if there is any at all, will be spasmodic and unreliable. The illusory seduction that we must consume for 'the benefit of all' will be a difficult line to sell for quite some time to come, if ever again.

Rather than being a year for recovery to start in the old sense, 2010 is better seen as the beginning of the end of the old obsessions with simplistic technology and rule by 'experts', who, after all, clearly do not know what is best. 2010-12 will see the last of the outer planets established in their new signs. By the end of this sub-period, all will be ready for a recovery into a very different world economy. Whether we experience it as heaven or hell will depend upon our understanding of the astro-cycles and the wisdom of our resultant actions.

Pluto in Capricorn — not intrinsically good or bad
This stage in the planet's cycle will be hard for people only to the extent they and the world economy reacted irresponsibly to Pluto's 1995-2008 transit through Sagittarius. Being too negative and defeatist about the change would be as wrong as it was to be over-optimistic during Sagittarian times. Happiness comes from understanding a cycle and so benefiting from it. There is no need to be despondent and miserably at its mercy. There must be a limitation on limitation. Rather, welcome the chance to balance the pattern of life. Be pleased to

have the space to do what it seemed there would never be time for.

Pluto's times in Capricorn over the past 500 years have seen important changes that have sired progress in subsequent decades and centuries. Chapter 8 showed 1516-32 bringing radical social change and the legitimacy of authority challenged. The years 1762-77 gave birth to modern industrial democracy and wide-ranging precise global measurements. These two stages together enabled individuals to break free from domination, to discover, learn, explore and create.

The current Pluto in Capricorn transit is the next stage — one that will integrate the ancient and modern. By understanding the astro-cycles we can develop tools of discriminating awareness to temper our power along much more appropriate and sustainable pathways.

The chapters that follow will study the astro-cycles of the period and some sub-periods in detail. They will consider the best and worst ways to handle the challenges and possibilities. These times could well see extremes of good or ill.

The 2010-12 transition

In April 1930 the Dow had struggled to recover from the 198 bottom on 13 November 1929 to top at 294 – just 92 points below its September 1929 all-time high. As spring turned to summer, and then autumn, a T-square in cardinal signs that had been between Pluto in Cancer, Saturn in Capricorn and Mars/Uranus in Aries was joined by Mars and Jupiter moving on to conjunct Pluto in Cancer. By mid-September the price was down to 234. From here its downward momentum was unstoppable until it reached below 42 in July 1932. July 2010 is the month when many stimulus-package supporting pundits insist the 'green shoots' must surely have come. As we have seen, at the end of this month there will be a cardinal T-square between Mars/Saturn in Libra, Pluto in Capricorn and Jupiter/Uranus in Aries. Compare the cycles and beware of placing too much reliance on any recovery being underway at that time.

In fact, Jupiter and Uranus retrograde back into Pisces, the former does not finally establish itself in Aries until January 2011. It is joined by Uranus in March. Neptune makes its first entrance at the beginning of Pisces in early April that year, returning to Aquarius between August and early February 2012. Seeing technological advance and scientific expertise as the essential foundation of a brilliant new society will begin to seem insufficient, jaded and out-dated through these transitional years.   This does not mean that the achievements of the past 300 years will be rejected and cast aside, rather that they will be put in perspective and appreciated for what they are not as well as what they are. We will acknowledge what material advances can do, but increasingly realise that their scope to satisfy is limited.

Basing policy on a developing framework of piecemeal, ever-changing statistical findings alone is far less reliable and far more dangerous than at first it might appear. It can even be unscientific. Jupiter holds back in Pisces, as if to prepare the way for Neptune to reside in there until the mid-2020s.   The need to feel sympathy, experience intimate contact and genuine understanding will now seem much more important. This will replace a set of politically correct rules, decided by strangers, who aim to protect people from themselves and control them by lowest common denominator judgements. Exploring personal wishes, rather than imposing rules-and-regulations strategies, could heal the left over angst created by well intentioned, but insensitive, Aquarian 'experts'.

Instead of new mechanical discoveries, the focus will turn to how we can use and maintain the equipment we have — especially what emerged over the past two decades. What we communicate and create by using mobile phones, the internet and the digital entertainment system, not the empty distraction of their use, will become far more important. We will seek to understand each other, to link and know innovative wonder. We will wish to be inspired — not jaded and bored by technological shells that may be brilliantly conceived but are empty of real substance.

Virgo Regulus Royal Star and economic recovery

The light of Regulus is among the brightest in the heavens. Appropriately, for well over two millennia[24] its Tropical zodiac sign position has been Leo. From 1237 UT on 28 November 2011 precession moves it on to Virgo. Embellishing this once-in-an-aeon change are the ingresses into Pisces, the exact opposite side of the zodiac, of the centaur Chiron and the planet Neptune[25]. On 19 April 2010, Chiron opposes Regulus, then at the very end of Leo, and enters Pisces the next day. On 20/21 July retrogression takes it back to Aquarius and a second opposition, and then on 8 February 2011 it makes its third and final opposition and ingress. Neptune performs a similar pattern on 4 April 2011, 5 August 2011 and 3 February 2012. By the time of the final ingress, Regulus is established in Virgo.

What does all this mean? The idealistic expression of Virgo (Regulus' new sign) is the material manifestation of pure, ineffably absolute perfection. The sign opposing it, Pisces, symbolises that deep ineffably intimate understanding that comes from taking the suffering of others upon oneself. It is across this opposition that the absolute ideals of the Virgin and Christ Jesus, her Son, are expressed.

Of course, only the most selfless and spiritually mature can express themselves at such a high level. For most of us, Virgo is experienced as flashes of purity amidst a constant striving to get things right and self-castigation for failing to do so. With Pisces we struggle between a natural inclination to offer constant sympathy and support and the feeling that we are not appreciated. The latter can degenerate into self-pity and resentment.

With these two archetypes taking the place of the Aquarius/Leo axis, idealism will move on to focus upon cleansing standards of care and propriety. The behaviour of the first decade will be considered cheap, coarse and unfeeling. Any attempts, during 2008-11, to return to that decade will appear facile and irresponsibly misconceived. Judgement when there is hurt in Pisces and a lowering of standards as seen from Virgo can be severe, even brutal. Many things will have been done and such dire consequences experienced that it will be difficult to forgive. The more that people dwell on such things, the more difficult it will be to find solutions.

The answer is to focus on the ideal and have the courage to face what has to be done to achieve it. These are the years when the wise will realise the sense in not wanting what we do not have to have; that the solution to the planet's ecological problems coincides with its peoples' genuine economic needs. We need and can be happier with far less and can support each other far more. Once again, let us be clear, growth is not the solution. Achieving the right quality of life and interaction with each other is far more important. If we are wise, these will be the years when humanity sees purity as our essence and recognises Saturn's vital role in its discovery.

Ecology and the economy share same interests

As we use our technology more to care better for each other, we can also use it more effectively to care for the planet. Scientific screening of ecological progress, measuring what we are taking from and giving to the eco-system, is just a start. We need to develop the skill and sensitivity to measure the full give-and-take impact of every activity and enterprise. Our accountants should be employed, not to marginalise risk away from the self-interest of those that pay their fees, but rather to cost in and integrate risk as broadly and completely as possible. Then we will know and pay the true cost of everything we do.

This would lead to genuine efficiency; decisions that benefit and so gain the support of more and more people. If we wish to build an airport, we cost in the effects. We do not see Britain's future in the world solely in terms of employment and profit, but in a higher role that does not harm quality of life, create social deprivation and health problems.

We attract tourists by making Britain a beautiful place, not just a busy one. With lateral thought, we may find more creative and exciting ways to build income. As material activities slow down, we may discover deeper, more effective, less competitive ways to know and work together with people from all over the world. As conflict dies down, perhaps we can divert our war industry towards feeding and healing the deprived — not exploiting them for their resources.

Regulus — falling to even worse economic failure

Such a positive vision of mutual understanding and sympathetic support is a natural development, but it will only be possible to the extent that we are willing to embrace the change. For all its bright splendour, built into the imagery of Regulus is the ongoing curse of kings: as rapid is the rise to glory, so rapid can be the fall from grace, with all power and glory gone.

As in 2008-9, we may refuse real change — even fight against it. The more we do, the more difficult and painful will be the consequences. Barriers will appear at every turn. Not accepting the real cause for these obstacles, we will argue, blame and dispute with others. Remember again, Saturn brings limitation to teach the consequences. Accepting and learning this can lead to great benefit. If you do not, the results can be harsh and unyielding.

Pisces, when combined with cardinal Aries, Capricorn and Saturn in Libra, can turn negative. In dire circumstances, self-pity can lead to blaming others for our predicament. Resentment can intensify into a desperate feeling that self-destructive martyrdom is the only way to salvation. An insane blame culture could then fragment societies. Vendettas caused by impulsive actions motivated by retribution could proliferate. As we seek to control what we feel is falling apart, societies could fragment into isolated acts of desperate authoritarian protection of the wealth that sub-groups have salvaged. The suffering of poor sub-groups, even entire disadvantaged countries, could become increasingly difficult to resolve, as debts remain unpaid and resources and services are all the more difficult to maintain. Those in power could be defensive, their accusations and answers to problems ever more unreasonable. People could become unyielding and insistently frozen upon their own 'solutions'. As willingness to let go of our positions and admit and learn from our errors diminishes, so will any hope for intelligent, meaningful change. All then will fall apart into 'every person for themselves' sub-groups.

Do not be deceived by an illusory 'middle' way

Even more likely is a third alternative. This is a middle way that this time will be far from the best option. Beware of a repetition of what happened in 1930-2, mentioned earlier in this chapter. Blind to all danger, we mistake a partial recovery for a real one, when the vital ground work is yet to be done. This could easily happen, because, as we have seen, the solutions to world economic crisis in 2009 are being muted by the same people and based on the same ideas that created crisis in the first place.

Imagine just about every 'quick trick' to 'restore confidence', build up asset values and 'get the show on the road' continues to be attempted. Governments still borrow enormous sums, print money, and accept liabilities they do not have the resources to cover. Any positive statistic is then laced with claims of 'green shoots of recovery'. With Jupiter hovering between Pisces and Aries until it enters Taurus in mid 2011 and Neptune hanging back in Aquarius until February 2012, it will be difficult to let go of hopes for a quick fix back to the past. Before a river finally dries up, there can be a deceptive moment when the water appears to rise. To mistake such temporary rising stock prices or growth in consumption as recovery could in the end make matters much worse.

For equity indices and other financial market data are ambivalent indicators of economic success and failure. Always bear in mind that all they really measure is how much money traders think they can make. Government intervention in markets with billions of dollars of investment can artificially create confidence, price growth and profits for traders. Should government regulate to block excessive rewards that do not benefit the real economy, the market may go down, because traders will lose. Mergers and takeovers usually lead to asset-stripping and job losses. This is bad news for staff, customers and suppliers — only the new owners really gain. So the stock price rises. Traders engage in financial markets to make money. Sustained boom times may point to periods when many people are experiencing wealth and plenty, but this is secondary to the real business in hand: professional traders at the cutting edge of the marketplace making far more for themselves.

With so much government money and guarantees propping up the system in 2009-10, 0 per cent interest rates and quantitative easing, by what criteria will we know when economies are really recovering — especially when employment rates tend to lag behind? With such strategies, sudden price improvements could prove to be no more than mini booms and busts. Inflation and increasing interest rates may not mean recovery, but be a crafty device to wipe out debt and devalue bank deposits.

Keep an eye on the markets, but beware of relying on them. In recent years, we have been concentrating too much on markets and not enough on why we have them. We go to supermarkets to buy what we need, but it is a sad life that focuses on nothing else. Shopping should be a nuisance we have to take care of. For most people economics, politics and even money itself should be like this. Life is for living, for art, for experience, for love and most of all for those convictions that make it all worthwhile.

Understanding consequences = right decisions
What happens will be a combination of all three options. That the future is always in our hands cannot be stated too often. Understanding the changing possibilities of each astro-cycle and using them wisely determines what will happen — be it for good or ill.

Saturn, the ruler of Pluto's sign (Capricorn) has, by its ongoing oppositions to Pluto, Neptune and Uranus, tracked the breakdown of the early 21st century's aimless techno-based world economy. With a pure and caring vision in place, it can now guide the rebuilding process. Basing structure upon sustainable economic expansion that regenerates itself by caring for the planet's eco-system will lead to sustainable success.

The solution lies beyond old flawed ideas and policies. It lies in much deeper understanding and far greater change. In Chapter 10, we will see that a genuinely sustainable world economy needs to be based upon a new 'Gold Standard'. We had better get this right. Chapter 11 shows clearly that in 2019 the astro-cycles will test us again and leave little room for manoeuvre.

Chapter 10
2012-18 — A Genuine Gold Standard

As soon as the world successfully navigated the Y2K hysteria and avoided the 'prophesied global destruction', cataclysm-watchers looked ahead to 2012. Could this year, when the Mayan calendar came to an end, be Armageddon[26]? Is such a question any more than a quaint human wish to live through momentous times? Is 21 December 2012 any more than the date when the Mayan people, studying a 5,000+ year period, stopped counting ahead?

Maybe not, but conscious of it or not, the expert Mayan astrologers certainly chose a significant year from the perspective of Western astrology. Not only does this year see the end of their macro-cycle based on a 260-day Venus-based calendar, but it comes at a settling time of many major outer-planetary sign changes and aspect connections. Astro-cycles change all the time but, as previous chapters have shown, in the decades since 1979 human consciousness has been bombarded by an extraordinary number of astro-events. From the second half of 2012, the outer planets will be more settled. The wise will step back; let the dust settle and hope to see clearly the best way ahead.

Although Uranus is in impulsive Aries, from 2012 it is balanced and tempered by Capricorn's ruler, Saturn, being in Libra and the practical realism of Jupiter in Taurus trining Pluto in Capricorn. In the autumn Saturn moves on to Scorpio to strengthen Neptune in Pisces. It is a good year to experience and assess the practical; to start to shape and mould new beginnings.

Learning from the past
To understand the importance of 2012 and the years immediately after, it is helpful to look back to the last time Uranus transited Aries. As already mentioned, this

was between 1928 and 1935 — the time of the Great Depression. By considering the similarities and differences between the two times, we may be able to anticipate how events could unfold in the 21st century and find a more positive process this time.

When Uranus previously entered Aries at the very beginning of 1928, it trined Neptune by sign, as long as the latter remained in Leo. So, its first influence was to encourage the mindless 'end-of-days' boom in stock prices leading to the October crash and the depression that followed. Since 1914, Pluto in Cancer had indicated the disruption of family and social foundations and the breaking down of many barriers to individual opportunity. With Neptune in Leo and Uranus in Pisces, not even prohibition had been able to quell the resultant self-indulgence. From July 1929, however, Neptune was fully established in detriment in Virgo. Then Uranus in impulsive Aries combined with it to trigger fanatically misguided counter reactions.

Neptune entering Virgo just before the Great Crash exacerbated resultant reactions of extreme guilt. Fanatical purist policies erupted and ran riot. The collapse of the German, Italian and Spanish economies and upsurge of Japanese colonialism led to Fascism and World War II. The collapse of the US and British economies led to Britain leaving the Gold Standard and Keynesian interventionist economics. World War II was followed in the UK by the counter of idealistic democratic socialism. All should have equal opportunity and ordinary people never suffer again as they had in the 1930s. War economies were transferred to peacetime mass-production of consumer goods. A period of indulgence produced petulant conflict and breakdown in the 1970s. In Chapter 4, we saw how this was answered by the simplistic market monetarism in the 1980s.

Yet, none of the developments over more than 50 years from 1929 achieved more than short-term opportunistic booms, followed by cutbacks, papered over with stop-gap solutions. All the time, we were using up, but not creating, resources. We were creating greater and greater imbalance in our relationships with the planet and each other. In direct contradiction to what it seemed like during recent prosperous times, we have never really dealt with the causes of the Great Depression. Does the downturn of 2008 and afterwards show we are yet to learn the lessons of the economic failure of the 1920s and 1930s?

Chapter 9 pointed to a more sustainable Virgo/Pisces purity than in the 1930s. With it, 2008-11 could see minds turn wisely forwards to a sensible future. It counselled against the danger of 'quick-fix' solutions. If we are still trying them in 2012, we will be suffering the consequences of the error of our ways. By then, we should at last be ready to consider radical alternative answers to economic issues that have been avoided for 100 years or more. Having experienced 80+ additional tumultuous years since 1929-35, now, in the 21st century, we have much more chance of finding better answers. To take full advantage of the opportunity of 2012, we really do have to ask whether anything that has been tried since 1929 is adequate or even correct. We have to question assumptions that in 2008 seemed sacrosanct.

* Was abandoning, rather than replacing the Gold Standard any more than an avoidance of reality?
* Do Keynesian-based stimuli only create short-term illusions of success that lead to bad economic judgements?
* Does government intervention based on social need lead to bureaucracy and lazy incompetence?
* Is an economy based on monetarist market forces impossibly impractical? For the policy to work, the banks, insurance companies, nations and depositors should have been subjected to the same 'rational market forces' faced by the 1980s UK miners and all privatised and taken-over industries.
* If monetarist free enterprise is not applied uncompromisingly, don't we create the worst of

all worlds — one of anarchistic greed, exploitation and resentment?

If experience suggests 'yes' to all these questions, clearly we need another way.

Where to turn for wise counsel?

What we face is the consequence of allowing decisions to be made for us by an unfettered unholy alliance. It is an alliance between those who control the financial, political and 'expert' scientific structures of society. Such experts stay in power by constantly compromising principles. They insist that what appears to be expedient has to hold sway over decency. The great ideal of a free enterprise world economy has turned out to be no more than a 'spiv culture' driven by greed and disregard for the happiness of whole nations and peoples. It has even marginalised and alienated family contacts and values.

Tighter systems of control on their own will not protect us from such dangers in the future. Indeed, they could well produce even worse centralised exploitation by those applying the rules[27]. The only reliable foundation combines the highest principles with common sense. An economic system that encourages people to want to do the right thing and leaves them freedom to do it their way is the only efficient system.

<u>The good news is that when Uranus and Neptune enter new signs in 2010-12, it is *after*, not before, an economic collapse</u>. In our present time, they are at a moment of solution, not cause. Uranus is in Aries, as before, but Neptune is in its ruling sign of Pisces, not in detriment in Virgo. This position should lead to contact and understanding; not alienating, ignorant, puritanical Fascism. The Cardinal T-square of 2010, explained in Chapter 9, comes not six months after the crash as in 1930, but 22 months after the 2008 collapse and 18 months after a new US President was elected rather than two years before[28]. Pluto is now in Capricorn — the opposite sign to Cancer. Combined positively with Neptune in Pisces, it symbolises authoritative

regeneration and realistic care. Its discipline can establish principles that set us free, provided these rules respect differences and are broadly, not selectively, sympathetic.

Discovering and defining a new Gold Standard

Pluto in Capricorn this time can provide the essential discipline needed for a sustainable world economy. By understanding the nature and time span of a particular astro-cycle, we know when, how and for how long is its influence. This creates a more effective economic model. We will move beyond boom/bust arguments over whether wealth should be distributed according to a trickle down, or bottom up model. The former fails because most people see wealth as existing to generate ever more for themselves. The later fails because it creates dependence. Clearly at the heart of a sustainable economy, we need a new Gold Standard. This time it will not be based on a yellow metal, for which the greedy fight and die. It will be rooted in a principle that all good people know in their heart of hearts makes sense — the principle outlined in Chapter 1 as the fundamental fact[29].

All our economic activities should be designed, assessed and controlled to 'balance the books' on every level of existence and experience. Economic theories to date have been no more than manipulative special pleadings. They have been used to ring-fence the facts in the interest of the sub-group believing in or paying for that way of looking at things.

In a truly sustainable economy all interests need to work in harmony; whether the wealth is going up or down becomes irrelevant. Instead, we seek intelligence and truth — something for something — nothing wasted at all levels and in all directions. The notion of a banker or trader manipulating a bonus system for personal gain would be seen and treated as criminal — no different to bank robbery. To harm others for commercial gain would be brute vandalism. The manufacture and distribution of weapons would be seen as an unfortunate necessity to be placed in as few hands as possible and so carefully controlled — not a way of keeping people in work. For resources to be under-priced, especially in areas of the world where poverty exists, would incur a levy automatically paid to the local community. To harm the environment would be seen as no different to a physical assault on another human being. If there is unemployment, work would be created by investing to divert surplus capacity to feed human need.

Illogical attempts to gain something for nothing have caused the failure of just about every aspect of financial market-based economies in their final years. The ingenuity of the bonus-seeking traders may serve their self-interest well, but makes no other logical market sense. Why gamble with options on commodities or possibilities you have no intention of obtaining? Why buy and sell shares intra-day, or for any short-term, purely financial, interest? A futures contract is invaluable to producers and manufacturers, but its operation should be confined to people genuinely engaged in the actual supply-and-demand marketplace. Speculative carpet-baggers and anyone who seeks to take advantage and cause suffering for personal gain should be excluded. In a properly balanced world economy they would be regarded as badly as are paedophiles and murderers.

To institutionalise the fundamental financial fact and these consequent aspirations into an incorruptible working model will be the task that the astro-cycles challenge us to have ready by 2018. It will not be achieved by dreamy idealism, but by an expansive structure of measurable principle. A helpful starting point comes from the insurance industry — the concept of insurable interest. What we give and take, stand to gain and lose must be measured. Yet, while the criteria of intrinsic value we adopt will be precise, this precision must centre around principle, not another set of rules and assumed values to get around. The constant interplay of legislation, techniques of avoidance and more legislation will not do at all. We need to encourage a higher standard of human behaviour. The public outrage against UK politicians was felt because the public had assumed their representatives understood it was the principle laying behind the rules (not the rules themselves) that was all-important. We must accept and embrace the principles of the new system generously, as we accept and embrace donating to charity appeals. To break a rule to sustain a principle may be acceptable; to betray a principle and use a rule to avoid the consequences or gain personal advantage would be totally unacceptable. Not to want the new 'Gold Standard' to work will be to want to be outside of all that is decent.

Computerising the Gold Standard

Modern computer technology, with its intricate interconnected systems, has ideal economic tools to build a viable business structure from given principles and values.   The concept of genuine intrinsic value we programme into the system must answer human and planetary ecological needs. Ethical principles must be established and adhered to by anyone devising and managing such a system. Not only *can* they not, but they would not wish to manipulate the system for personal reward. Their approach towards the principles would be no different than a doctor's commitment to his Hippocratic Oath. As doctors should not kill patients, so accountants should not cheat society — whether or not their actions are within the rules. Aspiring constantly to improve situations, people will always be ready to give more than asked, if it leads to genuine, lasting benefit. To the general public, manipulating such a system for person gain would be as unacceptable as today we see the 19th century practices of public hanging, torture and child cruelty.

The only acceptable exchange measure would represent genuine giving and taking. Actions would increase in value as the benefit of an activity is maximised. Benefit would be measured in terms of ecological, human and social need, as well as the materials and work involved in production. This new Gold Standard would establish a minimum base value, but the emphasis would be upon this value ever-growing. The wish to give more than asked would be more and more common, because we are motivated by the happiness of others and the realities of living on the planet. Crucially, it would be this enhanced prized value of the unit that we focus around, not rules and laws enforced by an authoritarian hierarchy and its legal advisers. Our 'currency' would be centred upon the measure of trust and freedom that enables diversity — the notion of giving without counting the cost, of giving more than is asked. This is the way to genuine, lasting economic success.

How much more satisfying this would be than recent business practices that sacrificed personal, social and international relationships to an ever-increasing empty obsession with gaining monetary advantage in purposeless business and exchange! With Pisces and Capricorn now the dominant energy, the style, art and experience of life will be a much higher priority. Responsible order and secure care will be more highly regarded than the presumptuous get-rich-quick tricks of the first decade of the 21st century.

Avoiding the alternative worse case scenario

Of course, such an idealistic vision, while the best way to utilise the astro-energy of these years, may not be what happens at all. The hard lessons of the transition from 2009 may not be learned. In 2010-12, we may have taken the negative or middle paths outlined in Chapter 9. If so, in the build up to 2015 and immediately after, with Uranus in Aries, Saturn entering Sagittarius and Jupiter in Leo, a return to market speculation could well gather pace. Read the next chapter to see why any initial optimism is likely to be short-lived.

It could be even worse if the world economy descends into protectionism, blame and conflict over resources, both between and within countries. Then Uranus in Aries and Neptune in Pisces could express themselves in manic persecution complexes between Pluto-in-Capricorn driven conflicting orthodoxies. Vendettas will be fuelled by each side remembering only the harm inflicted upon themselves and remaining insensitive to the harm they have done to others. As emotions and resentment build, desperate attempts to close ranks, put up barriers that 'protect against enemies' will proliferate. If we cannot understand differences and cooperate to answer each other's needs, nothing will be left to protect us. Instead there will be the violent conflict caused by the impulsive and unreasonable harshness with which we condemn what we do not understand.

Jupiter squaring Saturn in Leo/Scorpio between July 2014 and August 2015 and in Virgo/Sagittarius between August 2015 and September 2016 could be critical periods. If we have not learnt wisdom, we will struggle over resources and then blame and resent. Even if new systems are coming into place, a residual inclination towards market speculation could sorely test them.

It is a matter of choice

The cosmic and ecological facts make this a time of extremes. We either get it right or enter a major cycle of disaster from which many people may not survive. To avert this, for once and for all we need to accept that all strategies to bounce the world economy to 2007 boom levels will fail for very logical reasons. No one is to blame. Our desperate 2008-9 initiatives were much too unrealistic to be possible. Now in 2012 and ever after, we must accept that the worse will continue to happen until we change to a sustainable economic model. .

Rebuild every element of the world economy on a foundation of honesty, decency and common sense give and take. In the first half of the 21st century, we need to outlaw exploitation, manipulation and self-interest to the same extent that the second half of the 20th century sought to outlaw sexism, racialism, genocide and torture. We should tax growth based on greed and unkindness to people and places. We should encourage and invest in growth that empowers others to be peaceful and happy. Let us compete in how well we can answer each other's needs.

Many will say such ideas are impractical, idealistic — beyond the capacity of human nature. Is it suggested that in our advanced interactions between people and nations in the 21st century, common sense is impossible?

The furore over standards in public life, occurring in Britain in 2009, reveals a thirst in favour of principle before rules and regulations. Opinion leaders, who find a meaningful way of articulating and applying golden standards, will find they are tapping into a rich vein of public support.

Chapter 11
2019-2024 — The Time of Reckoning

Not steering by the venal chart
That tricked the mass for private gain,
We rise to play a greater part...
Men shall know commonwealth again..'
**Leonard Cohen: from 'Villanelle for our
Time', *Dear Heather*[30].**

While Pluto remains in Capricorn and Neptune in Pisces, in May 2018 Uranus navigates the cusp of Taurus and will be fully established there by March 2019. At the very end of 2017 Saturn enters Capricorn to be joined by Jupiter in early December 2019. From then until the 2020 Vernal Equinox and again between July and December 2020, four out of the five outermost planets are in earth signs.

Earth stellia and major market downturns
Any group of planets forming a stellium in earth signs frequently indicates major consolidation in the financial markets. In greed-based economies, it has often indicated a top that remains unbroken for a considerable time. Prices go sideways or descend rapidly. In December 1989, six planets in Capricorn called the 38,951 top of the Japanese Nikkei. It was soon less than half this level. Even during the 1990s boom it could only recover above 20,000 intermittently and has traded much lower since April 2000, reaching down to 7000 during the 2008 crisis. In January 1994, a similar stellium in Capricorn was at a top in world bond and equity markets. In the spring of 2000, seven planets in another earth sign, Taurus, were at a top of the most substantial equity price boom to date, driven mainly by new technology stocks.

Looking further back, the August 1720 crash in South Sea Company stock came in a month when there were up to five planets in earth signs, including Pluto in Virgo and Neptune in Taurus. Since the late 18th century start of our market records, Jupiter, Saturn, Uranus and

Pluto have rarely been in earth signs at the same time. When they were for roughly twenty weeks from early December 1853, the index of US stocks fell from 21.13 to 17.67, after which the price was to continue downward to reach 8.33 in July 1859. The second occasion, the year from April 1881, formed a price plateau, from which there was a 18 per cent fall by December 1884. The month from 1969 was a top before a drop.

Jupiter, Saturn and Pluto in Capricorn, with Uranus in any earth sign, has not and will not occur at any time between 2500 BC and 5000 AD except for the three and a half months from December 2019 and five and a half months from early July 2020 mentioned above. Indeed, the only previous time between AD 1000 and 2500 that Jupiter, Saturn and Pluto have been in Capricorn together was for two months from November 1284. As well as being when Edward I incorporated Wales into England, it was the year that the Republic of Venice began coining the gold ducat. This was to become the standard European coin for 600 years. 26 June that year is the legendary date on which the Pied Piper used the enchantment of his pipe to lead 130 children astray into a mountainside trap — not a bad analogy for what happens at the end of a boom!

In 2019 there will be the 246-year Pluto return of the Boston Tea Party that was to lead to American Independence. We have seen in Chapter 8 that 2009-24 is the first time that Pluto has returned to Capricorn since the start of the Industrial Revolution. When Jupiter and Saturn enter Capricorn to join Pluto, they will test, as did Pluto in 2008-9, the 1984 Capricorn ingress of Jupiter/Neptune. As we saw in Chapter 4, this combined with Uranus in Sagittarius to inspire the 1980s vision of an electronic, free market economy, with all the consequences that this study has explored.

2019/20 – unshakeable reality

For many reasons, 2019-20 and the years that follow will confront the world economy with reality. Any pretence of recovery and growth that is not strongly based and sustainable will top and fade away. Attempting to force and bully success at the expense of others will meet with insurmountable barriers. As with the ducat, only a genuine unit of value that is acceptable and valuable to all is likely to be recognised and to last. This time we will need more than a symbolic metal. Anything that can be held by some at the expense of others will not be good enough. We need now the 'currency' with the excellent qualities described in the previous chapter, one that measures not just the value of what we possess, but the entire intention and effect of our endeavours. If we are to make a genuine breakthrough out of 2009's broken confusion to a happier new world, it would not be too fanciful, indeed it would be eminently appropriate, to call the new unit of currency 'a kindness'.

In seeking to look so far ahead from the time of writing, it is important to let go of attachment to what we now assume to be essential. What can be said for sure is that the astro-cycles focused upon 2019 symbolise unavoidable reality. There will be no room to manipulate the truth. If we get it wrong, the consequences will be uncompromisingly harsh. To get it right, it may be necessary to use very different methodology to assess reality. Obsession with financial market price levels may have become outdated or sidelined. As mentioned earlier, the rise and fall of financial markets is dependent upon perceived profitability. Easy gains create booms. The markets being high are a sign that traders expect easy gains. In an ecologically sensitive, broadly balanced give and take, genuine 'gold' standard (kindness) based economy, over-inflated financial market prices, the very boom tops celebrated as economic success in 2007, could well be considered very bad news.

The worst that could happen
What happens will depend on whether in the second decade of the 21st century we have the wisdom and courage to learn from the failings of the first. Since the late 17th century, economic and political relationships

have been grounded increasingly upon the valuation and exchange of currencies, commodities, shares and other symbolic assets. These means of exchange have become ever more abstract from the realities they represent. The study of economics has emerged as a convenient way to involve more and more people in amoral relationships. Maybe the 2010s will see the brightest minds focused on propping up the market economy and finding ways of 'kicking into touch' ecological and social realities. It may seem as the decade develops that, at the expense of considerable hardship for many, the world economy is riding the storm and we are on course for a price recovery — 'in which all will share in time'. We would be deluded to think so. If we have not learned from the consequences of the 1720 and 1835, 1929 and 2008 booms and busts, the powerful reality of the earth focus of 2019 could be the rudest awakening of all, as economies top and fall yet again.

A worse possibility could be that world social relationships are in such a state of crisis that the economic consequences are not the major part of the problem. The 1930s Depression was followed by World War II. By 1940, there was an earth stellium with Jupiter, Saturn and Uranus in Taurus and Neptune in Virgo. The 1989 stellium in Capricorn, opposed Jupiter in Cancer, saw not only an economic recession but also the breakdown of the Soviet system. The Iraqi invasion of Kuwait the following year sired a new dimension in global terrorism. It is the reaction to this that is creating a whole new relationship between governments and their citizens.

If the actions taken to resolve the 2008 economic downturn have been impulsive, ill-considered and especially insensitively authoritarian, then 2019 could be a dire year for global relationships and individual freedom. As so many people are warning, we may by then really have sleep-walked into a world based on the template of George Orwell's *1984*: a world of two or three intransigent power blocks in a constant state of war with each other.

In such a world, the complete absence of understanding, respect and trust leads to relationships based on absolute hatred. Because of this constant threat to their society's way of life, individual citizens are carefully scrutinised to ensure their work and thoughts are focused correctly. In such a society, the allocation of money and resources is centrally controlled and the true relationship between events, actions and outcomes never understood. The individual is seen entirely as existing to serve the central needs of society. This is the most unenlightened, yet a highly possible, use of Jupiter, Saturn and Pluto in Capricorn with Uranus in Taurus.

The best that could happen

At the opposite end of the spectrum of possibility is the use of these astro-cycles in the most efficient, creative and effective way possible. We melt away fear by serving each other and the planet. We do not accept that blame lies far away, due to ways and beliefs we do not understand. We demand to be free and to decide for ourselves. We reject the dark path of never-ending fear that leads to slavery. We also reject the inefficient second best and impotent compromise of a manipulated market economy.

Rather than manipulated and deceptive price levels, the genuine test as to whether our world and our lives are performing well is to look at the extent of conflict both within societies and between them. Are there wars and terrorist threats? How many people remain hungry and ill? Are lifespans longer for more people? Are such happy lives distributed more evenly across the planet than in the first decade of the 21st century? Is pollution diminishing? Has political communication become less manipulative? Are economic growth and wealth seen as far less important and now looked upon as secondary servants of human need? Are we feeling better and becoming well?

At the negative extreme, the control of market price levels would be in the hands of a hidden elite. Such a system would use the earth outer planetary stellium to impose systems that bear down upon the people. If old market price manipulation remains a part, levels will halt and be corrected downwards. Consequent problems will be blamed on scapegoats.

By contrast, at the positive extreme, an economy based on a proper, kind Gold Standard of transparent people participation would welcome the stellium as a touchstone of order and efficiency – a genuine test of the co-creative relationship between humanity and the planet.

Preparing for Pluto in Aquarius

With Saturn ingressing back and forth across the cusp of Aquarius between March and June 2020, the earth stellium starts to unravel. In January/February 2021, Saturn is joined by Jupiter and both square Uranus in Taurus. With Saturn staying in Aquarius until 7 March 2023 and Pluto making its first ingress in that sign on 23rd March 2023, only 16 days later, we will come out of the 2019 stellium ready to see Saturn very differently.

Change is the lesson of astro-cycles. So these last three to four years of Pluto's transit through Capricorn are best used as a preparation for its next change of sign. Just as it was dangerously counter productive to hang on to Sagittarius between 2004 and 2008, when we should have been preparing for Capricorn, so in 2020-24, we need to look ahead. With Jupiter and Saturn preparing the ground, it should be a more natural development this time. Pluto will be moving from a deterministic to a systematic implementation of Saturn. Such a transition should seem a natural opening out, rather than, as in 2008-9, a coming off of the Jupiterian rails and confronting Saturn's rules.

So do we return to Aquarian times and all that technology? Yes, in a way, but after 10 or more years of realistic restructuring, with a three to four year run in to adjust, the technology will be very different. Also, Neptune remains in Pisces until 2025 and Uranus in Taurus until the year after that. If we have restructured wisely the transition to Pluto's ingress into Aquarius should be a conscious opening out to a more ordered world society.

Of course, we may not have been that sensible. Read ahead and consider the possibilities.

Chapter 12
Towards a Genuine Age of Aquarius?

'Every nation, culture, religion and philosophy already has a heritage of wisdom. We can use this wisdom to create a universal education.' **Lama Thubten Yeshe**

As Pluto enters the new sign astrologers will be either regretting an opportunity lost or celebrating the fruits of a long haul towards a disaster averted. For now the kind of lives and world we have created for ourselves while Pluto transited Capricorn will determine how we experience its transit through Aquarius. To understand and be more specific ahead of the time, we need to consider the role of science and technology in society.

Science and technology in a future society

By emasculating human commonsense, the overriding dominance of science and technology in the decades leading to 2008 was a major contributing cause of the economic downturn. The condition of human society as Pluto entered Capricorn saw:

* Technology for little purpose, except its own sake.
* The dominance of mechanical science over human nature and creativity.
* An information-obsessed academia.
* An expert-driven society advising 'lesser beings' as to 'their best interests'.
* The seduction of science by business interests.
* The breakdown of friendship, causing fear that seemed to justify intensive surveillance.
* The consequent retreat from natural human wisdom and decency.

Paradoxically, once these errors are corrected and individuals become their own authority again, existing inventions — and far more advanced ones — can and will play proper important roles in world society.

So, it is appropriate to end this economic study of the period Pluto occupies Capricorn, with a consideration of a genuinely sustainable Aquarian technological archetype. Also, to point to a dire warning should proper human control of the relationship between science, technology and the planet not be achieved by this time.

Learning from *Star Trek*

The *Star Trek* television series fantasises a remarkable economic structure. Set in the 24th century, it describes an Earth where computer and manufacturing technology is so advanced that material hardship is a thing of the past. As a result of extensive space travel, based on 'warp' technology producing speeds several times that of light, its citizens have joined with those from other populated planets to explore and expand knowledge of an ever-widening Universe.

Our 20th/21st Century notion of economic growth and profit is satirised by an alien race called the Ferengi. This self-obsessed and self-indulgent people with ludicrously large and highly sensitive ears abide by *The 285 Rules of Acquisition*. Earthly and most other races view them with an amused, patronising disdain. When you can have all you need and wish for, why base your life and personal pride on the struggle to have more?

The symbolism is profound. In this highly advanced 24th century technological world almost anything is available on request and you can teleport to new places in an instant. Yet <u>it is a decision of character that determines what is important in our lives</u>. It is not necessary to wait for conditions to be right to get the quality of our lives and relationships right. Rather, by having the vision, we can invent the technology to provide our dreams.

Our negative, selfish and short-sighted minds created an experience of constant fear and hardship, as we consumed plenty during the first decade of the 21st century. Yet at any time, if we believe or wish for kinder and more generous outcomes, we can control our minds to work and make it so.

The influence of the *Star Trek* fantasy on our lives in the 20th and early 21st centuries is well documented. Martin Cooper, who is thought to be the inventor of the first mobile phone, claims to have been inspired by watching Captain Kirk using his communicator on *Star Trek*[31]. The series inspired many other inventions, such as MIT's Tractor Beam, the University of Washington's Tricorder, US Air Force's transparent armour, Vocera's Communications System's hands-free and voice-activated device for users to talk with co-workers. Even phaser guns, cloaking devices, hypersprays and more are under development[32].

The limited introduction of such technology to date has already led to dramatic changes in the way we work together and our power to change our circumstances. Could it be that the disgrace of the 'captains' of our contemporary material world, due to the economic and political collapse from 2008-9, opens the door to our finding an ethical foundation for the future? By 2024, will such a foundation have become strong enough to contain and sustain an economy that includes replication and transportation of anything anywhere we wish? Almost certainly not, but it helps to see that we may be going that way in the centuries ahead. Compare the progress made in the last 100 and then 300 years.

More lessons to learn first?

There are very good astrological reasons for placing such a *Star Trek* economy in the 24th century. For, according to most astronomical calculations, this is the century when the Precession of the Equinoxes leads to the Vernal Equinox point moving from sidereal Pisces to Aquarius[33]. According to most authorities, in 2024 we will still have 360+ years to go. Realising this puts the technological developments of the 20th/21st centuries changeover in perspective. Far from being the new Age of Aquarius, it was a false dawn. It did no more than reveal just how much we have to learn about ourselves and our organisations. We need to advance considerably to master and enjoy the freedoms that a genuine Aquarian

Age would bring. With Jupiter, Neptune and Chiron in a very rare close transit through Aquarius, from mid-2009 is a unique opportunity to visualise an idealistic future[34]. Maybe a spark from then will grow and light the way.

It is worrying, however, that, writing between the 1960s and 1990s and looking forward, the *Star Trek* creators saw a 21st century war. They postulated a horrific conflict to teach humanity to question and change social principles. It needed such a harsh lesson to focus society on a kind heart core. This core would start it on a path where it became capable of being the focal centre of an enlightened Federation of Planets. To date we have done the opposite. We have combined the events of 9/11, our hubris to create without responsibility, and our greed to consume, into a justification for a seemingly endless war on terror and economic anarchy that threatens the destruction of our planet.

This study has suggested that Pluto's transit through Capricorn offers a last-ditch opportunity to correct these errors. The vision of a new and sustainable Gold Standard based upon kindness is the antidote that can be established and tested by the time Pluto enters Aquarius. This would regenerate and manage our new economy and inspire respect and trust between peoples and religions. It would lead to a lessening of demand and relax the pressure on the planetary eco-system. Only when we have ethical, balanced respect for each other would replication technology be capable of introduction without social disaster.

On the other hand, if we can see no further than tricking the planetary economy back to the illusion of boom and prosperity we were experiencing in the years leading to 2007-8, we are doomed to the continual still-birth of short-term success. Lacking in the self-criticism and clear vision that regenerates for the future, consensus will fall apart as more and more countries and groups break ranks. Judgemental accusations and protectionism will fragment sympathy and understanding. Simplistic solutions of self-interest could then lead to war, which closed minds will struggle to escape from.

The worst of times

With Pluto in Capricorn and Saturn so dominant in other ways from 2009-24, if we focus upon power blocks, establish barriers and continue to develop armaments from modern technology, we could enable a very different and negative view of the Pluto in Aquarius period — death and transformation through technology. It is no accident that futuristic films depict the immediate future as being full of technological nightmares. Let us remind ourselves for a third time that the way out of the 1930s Depression was the 1940s World War II.

In the preface to this study, three alternative potential outcomes to any astro-cycle were identified. We could understand the potential of the times, take the strain, and then learn and apply the lessons to correct any problems we face. At the other extreme, we could react with mindless emotion and strike out to 'eradicate' the 'villains' we hold to be responsible for our problems. More likely is compromise; a piecemeal, pragmatic approach. By ignoring and manipulating, we avoid the issues and build up problems for the future. During the 2009-24 Capricorn time this option will be far less available. The problems have to be fully and properly addressed. In short, we need all the friends we can get. However different, even alien, others appear to be, we need to find ways to understand and respect them.

The best of times

Of course, the value of science fiction is not so much to predict the future as to write parables about the decisions we face in our own times. Even in the 24th century the wisdom of The Federation still leaves them in the midst of many uneasy conflicts, with the Klingons, Romulans, Borg and a horrific life-draining war with the Dominion. Each side's approach to such conflicts reinforces the very lessons we have to learn. The suffering that ensues is always caused by the ego: the belief that an individual or particular group is more important than the interests and happiness of all other creatures. Those that turn away from this with a smile know this. Those than frown face another cycle of suffering before they will have another opportunity to learn and be happy.

However the world finds itself as Pluto transits Aquarius, it will be around this basic distinction that a future wise study of the way forward will turn.

Appendix

The Key Concepts of Mundane Astrology

To grasp the full impact of the significance and usefulness of the astro-cycle combinations in this study, a basic understanding and experience of astrology is needed. For readers not familiar with the subject, below is an introduction to the main planet and zodiac sign meanings of the outer planets, plus some simple insights into how astrologers combine them.

This introduction focuses on the five outer-planets used in mundane financial and historical astrology. A full beginners' appendix, with all the main planets and their workings, can be found at the end of *Astrology and Compassion the Convenient Truth* by Roy Gillett[35]. This book explains how astrology works, might be researched and answers many popular criticisms. It gives an incisive introduction to the incredible value of astrology in personal and social life, economic and otherwise.

The astrology chart

To measure the positions and relationships of the planets, we project the point on Earth we are studying outward, to infinity in every direction. This imagined infinite three-dimensional ball we call the celestial sphere. This is divided into twelve segments known as the signs of the zodiac, named after the constellations nearest to them. We use these twelve signs to measure the positions of the Sun, Moon and planets from our Earthly (geocentric) perspective. We also note which signs are on the horizons and the higher and lower meridians as the Earth spins on its axis.

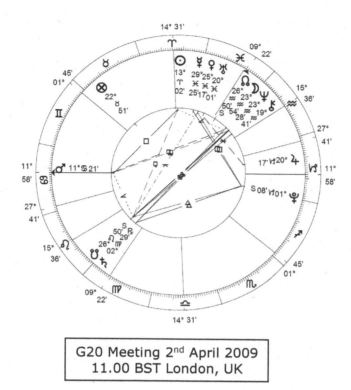

G20 Meeting 2nd April 2009
11.00 BST London, UK

These three-dimensional movements are simplified to a flat chart. Above is a full chart is drawn for the start of the 2009 G20 meeting in London, discussed in Chapter 8 — see pages 55-6.

* The outer band shows the twelve signs of the *zodiac*.
* The *planets*, whose symbols are inside the zodiac band, move at varying speeds around the zodiac in an anti-clockwise direction. The Moon changes sign every two and a half days. Pluto can take more than twenty years to change sign because its orbit is so much bigger.
* The lines that connect the planets across the centre of the chart are called the *aspects*.

The sections that follow explain the timings of the planetary cycles, the meanings of these planets, the zodiac signs they occupy and the aspects they make to each other.

The timings of the planetary cycles

The first principle of astrology is to remember we live upon and observe the Universe from the Earth. Although named after nearby star constellations, the signs of the zodiac are patterns projected upon the heavens from the Earth — rather as we look the other way and project time zones on the Earth's surface to show different clock times around the world.

We project the zodiac on the heavens so we can have a reference frame upon which to measure the apparent geocentric movements of the heavens — especially the planets of our solar system. We are familiar with the Moon's monthly cycle and the Sun's yearly one. Mercury and Venus, when observed from the Earth, appear to have erratic orbits that take roughly the same time to go around the zodiac as does the Sun. Mars takes two Earth years; Jupiter twelve, changing sign once a year; Saturn 29.5 years; Uranus 84; Neptune 165; and Pluto 246 years.

Due to the different lengths of orbit of the planets around the Sun, when observed from where we are on the Earth, at times these planets appear to be moving backwards against the zodiac background. This is called retrogression. The outer planets spend several months appearing to move backwards every year.

Also, because of the different lengths of their orbits around the Sun, when we mark planets' positions on the zodiac circle the degrees of the circle between them will change. Observation has shown astrologers that certain angles indicate planets will work easily with each other (120, 60, 30 degrees), whereas other angles indicate tension (45, 90, 135, 180). When planets are in the same position (conjunct), what they symbolise tends to combine — depending upon the planets — this can symbolise harmony, tension or both together. The time it takes for two outer planets to be conjunct (in the same place), opposed and conjunct again will vary. Jupiter and Saturn are conjunct every 20 years. Neptune and Pluto take 493 years to do the same. When more than two outer planets are involved or we look for aspects in particular signs, even longer historical cycles are produced.

The planets in the zodiac signs

Mundane astrologers study the relationship between planetary and zodiac meanings, handed down to us from thousands of years of study, alongside trends and events in history. This gives them insight into the timing of changes of attitudes and taste. It is these which in turn lead to the nature of the events.

What follows is an introduction to the key meanings of the planets and the 12 zodiac signs they can occupy. The Moon, Sun and inner planets are included for completeness. These tend to suggest monthly and yearly repeating cycles that are more to do with daily and personal, rather than historical, changes. However, by combining in a rare way or by linking with the outer planetary cycles, they can symbolise the triggering of remarkable historical events.

To simplify all this and make it usable for you right away, the meanings of the zodiac signs and planets have been reduced to the single keywords below.

Planet		Keyword	Sign		Keyword
☉	Sun	express	♈ Aries		urgently
☽	Moon	react	♉ Taurus		realistically
☿	Mercury	think	♊ Gemini		intelligently
♀	Venus	love	♋ Cancer		carefully
♂	Mars	act	♌ Leo		proudly
♃	Jupiter	expand	♍ Virgo		precisely
♄	Saturn	control	♎ Libra		adaptively
♅	Uranus	invent	♏ Scorpio		intensely
♆	Neptune	inspire	♐ Sagittarius		far-reaching
♇	Pluto	transform	♑ Capricorn		usefully
☊	Node	opportune	♒ Aquarius		knowingly
			♓ Pisces		sympathetically

Look at the G20 Meeting chart and combine the keywords of each of the planets and signs to make phrases. Now add some additional words associated with these keywords. When you have jotted down some ideas, compare them with the interpretation of the chart at the beginning of Chapter 8.

Of course, the signs and the planets have far richer meanings than can be expressed in one word. In the Planets and Zodiac sections that follow, a rich spectrum of possible[36] associations is listed for each of the outer planetary and all of the zodiacal archetypes. By synthesising these meanings we begin to understand the breadth and depth of the archetypes' potential to explain the nature of people and events.

The outer planets

Because they are common to the charts of people and events for a whole year (Jupiter) up to 20+ years (Pluto), these outer planets symbolise attitudes held and events experienced by all the people born during the periods of time the planets are in those signs. Teachers find that a whole year group will react to the same lesson differently from the previous year group. Attitudes of one generation are different from another. To see the astro-cycle foundation, we need to study the key ideas of the outer planets and then the twelve signs they pass through. As you do this, you will understand how I have come to make the statements earlier in this book. You may well develop the skill to adapt and improve them.

♃ Jupiter * King of the Gods * Lord of Light * the emperor * the judge * the teacher * number 3 * Thursday * purple * the tonic sol * smell * middle age * liver and pituitary * tin * sapphire, amethyst and turquoise * jasmine * nutmeg, sage, oak and poplar * the energy of expansion, generosity, how you expand.

♄ Saturn * Kronus * God of the World and Time * the politician * the businessman * number 8 * Saturday * black * the tonic re * hearing * old age * gall bladder, skin and bones * lead * jet, onyx and black diamond * musk, poppy seeds and cinnamon * thistle, camomile, yew, ash, alder, cypress * the energy of limitation, structure, how you control.

♅ Uranus * God of the Sky * Father of the Titans * the reformer * the revolutionary * mustard brown * the tonic do * inner sight, clairvoyance * pineal gland * circulation * copper * turquoise and malachite * the energy of awakening, sudden change, how you invent.

♆ Neptune * Poseidon, holding a trident * God of the Sea * the poet * the deceiver * dull grey to black * the tonic re * inner touch, psychometry * nervous systems * silver * rock crystal and opal * the energy of mysticism, how you inspire.

Pluto * Hades * God of the Underworld * the subconscious * atomic power * brown and maroon * the tonic mi * gonads, cell production and reproduction * iron * diamond, bloodstone topaz and agate * the energy of death and rebirth, how you transform.

The zodiac

The meanings of the signs the planets pass through are best understood by considering how they combine one of three key essential variable archetypes and their planetary ruler(s). Focusing these meanings together in our minds suggests one especially appropriate verb. All these concepts are given in **bold** at the beginning of the zodiac listing below.

Each sign is allocated just one alternative for each variable archetype, which are:

* ⁕ *Cardinal, fixed or mutable*: if one were mixing a cake, fixed would represent the bowl, mutable the malleable ingredients and cardinal the spoon.
* ⁕ *Fire, Earth, air, or water*: for existence to grow and develop, we need the ability to dream and plan (air), to implement (fire), create and own (earth), and make contact to enjoy and/or fear the consequences (water).
* ⁕ *Positive or negative*: creative, expressive and thrusting (positive) or receptive, assessing, drawing in (negative).

Aries * the Ram * cardinal * fire * positive * Mars * I am * the principle of ideation * God of Control * red * head and face * headaches and anger * Kali Phos cell salt * key of D flat * iron * bloodstone * fruit of all plants * pine and cypress * geranium, honeysuckle and nettles *all things of impulsive action, challenge, new beginnings.

Taurus * the Bull * fixed * earth * negative * Venus * I have * the principle of ingestion * God of Obedience * indigo * throat and neck * illnesses of colds and obesity * Nat Sulph cell salt * key of E flat * copper * sapphire * roots of all plants * ash tree * apple and beans * all things that bring fullness - the richness and beauty of the earth.

♊ **Gemini * the Twins * mutable * air * positive * Mercury * I think** * the principle of communication * God of Wisdom * yellow * nerves, shoulders, arms and lungs * asthma and nervous disorders * Kali Mur cell salt * key of F * mercury * emerald * flowers of all plants * nut-bearing trees * lavender and carrot * all things that bring quick thinking and communication.

♋ **Cancer * the Crab * cardinal * water * negative * Moon * I feel** * the principle of assimilation * God of Harmony * ice blue * chest and stomach * indigestion, ulcers and chronic diseases * Calc Fluor cell salt * key of A flat * silver * pearl * leaves of all plants * rubber and all trees rich in sap * flax and privet * all things that bring anxious care and nurturing of life.

♌ **Leo * the Lion * fixed * fire * positive * Sun *I will** * the principle of co-ordination * God of Gratitude * golden * heart and sensory nerves * fevers and heart attacks * Mag Phos cell salt * key of D * gold * ruby * seeds of all plants * citrus and palm trees * sunflower, marigold and walnut * all things that suggest glory and life-giving energy.

♍ **Virgo * the Virgin * mutable * earth * negative * Mercury *I analyse** * the principle of discrimination * God of Justice * brown * intestines, joints, nervous system * bowel troubles and spasms * Kali Sulph cell salt * key of C * mercury * sardonyx * roots of all plants * hazel and nut-bearing trees * corn * morning glory, caraway and myrtle * all things that suggest correction and perfect manifestation.

♎ **Libra * the Scales * cardinal * air * positive * Venus * I balance** * the principle of equilibrium * God of Reality * rose * kidneys * debility * Nat Phos cell salt * key of D * copper * sapphire * flowers of all plants * ash trees * lilac, garden mint and asparagus * all things that suggest harmony, acting with correct consideration.

♏ **Scorpio * the Scorpion/Eagle * fixed * water * negative * Mars and Pluto * I want** * the principle of regeneration * God of Vision * dark red * sexual and excretory organs * piles, ruptures, venereal disease * Calc Sulph cell salt * key of E * iron * opal * leaves of all plants * bushy trees * carnation, rhododendron, broom and tobacco * all things that suggest desire, passion and transformation.

Sagittarius * the Archer * mutable * fire * positive *
**Jupiter * I see ** the principle of projection * God of Victory *
purple * liver, hips and thighs * blood disorders, tumours *
Silica cell salt * key of F * tin * turquoise * ash and oak trees
* dandelions and moss * all things that suggest vision, activity and
generosity.

Capricorn * the Goat * cardinal * earth * negative *
**Saturn * I use ** the principle of regulation * God of Power *
black * knees and bones * rheumatism * Calc Phos cell salt *
key of G * lead * jet and onyx * roots of all plants * pine and
willow * hyacinth and onion * all things that limit, structure and control.

Aquarius * the Water Carrier * fixed * air * positive *
**Saturn and Uranus * I know ** the principle of association *
God of Love * turquoise * ankles and circulation * the illness
of varicose veins * Nat Mur (common salt) cell salt * key of A
* platinum and uranium * black pearl * flowers of all plants * most fruit
trees * orchid, daffodil and hemp * all things that stimulate change and
objectivity.

Pisces * the Fishes * mutable * water * negative * Jupiter
and Neptune * I believe and often suffer * the principle of
empathy * God of Mastery * soft sea greens * feet * illnesses
from impure blood, especially gout * Ferr Phos (iron) cell salt
* key of G flat * tin * amethyst * leaves of all plants * trees near water *
water lily, tulip and fig * all things sensitive, mysterious and the fullness of
experience.

Expanding planet-in-sign meanings

The rich store of meanings and associations in the Planets and
Zodiac sections give more colour to interpretation. Below are
some phrases for planets in signs created this way. By thinking
like a poet, these phrases can be added to and combined. We
can mould the concepts of the interaction of several planets
together into sentences, even paragraphs, of description.

Always remember that astrological qualities can be
negative as well as positive. Strong air can indicate a brilliant
mind, over-dependence on ideas, even neurosis. Dominant fire
suggests great will power, but can be over-bearing.

Planets in ARIES indicate you will

♃	Jupiter	expand bravely
♄	Saturn	control with difficulty
♅	Uranus	invent restlessly
♆	Neptune	inspire over-idealistically
♇	Pluto	transform powerfully

Planets in TAURUS indicate you will

♃	Jupiter	expand physically
♄	Saturn	control methodically
♅	Uranus	invent inappropriately
♆	Neptune	inspire indulgently
♇	Pluto	transform materialistically

Planets in GEMINI indicate you will

♃	Jupiter	expand without boundaries
♄	Saturn	control diligently
♅	Uranus	invent unreliably
♆	Neptune	inspire impressionably
♇	Pluto	transform unusually

Planets in CANCER indicate you will

♃	Jupiter	expand caringly
♄	Saturn	control uncertainly
♅	Uranus	invent social norms
♆	Neptune	inspire affectionately
♇	Pluto	transform society

Planets in LEO indicate you will

♃	Jupiter	expand imperially
♄	Saturn	control reliably
♅	Uranus	invent chancily
♆	Neptune	inspire without responsibility
♇	Pluto	transform forcefully

Planets in VIRGO indicate you will

♃	Jupiter	expand discursively
♄	Saturn	control correctly
♅	Uranus	invent with individual style
♆	Neptune	inspire fanatically
♇	Pluto	transform scientifically

Planets in LIBRA indicate you will

♃	Jupiter	expand with justice
♄	Saturn	control at all costs
♅	Uranus	invent conservatively
♆	Neptune	inspire romantically
♇	Pluto	transform nervously

Planets in SCORPIO indicate you will

♃	Jupiter	expand attractively
♄	Saturn	control reluctantly
♅	Uranus	invent dangerously
♆	Neptune	inspire deeply
♇	Pluto	transform totally

Planets in SAGITTARIUS indicate you will

♃	Jupiter	expand with vision
♄	Saturn	control by alienation
♅	Uranus	invent far-sightedly
♆	Neptune	inspire energetically
♇	Pluto	transform far-reachingly

Planets in CAPRICORN indicate you will

♃	Jupiter	expand responsibly
♄	Saturn	control strongly
♅	Uranus	invent resolutely
♆	Neptune	inspire thoroughly
♇	Pluto	transform dictatorially

Planets in AQUARIUS indicate you will

♃	Jupiter	expand with hope
♄	Saturn	expect self-control
♅	Uranus	invent progressively
♆	Neptune	inspire idealistically
♇	Pluto	transform co-operatively

Planets in PISCES indicate you will

♃	Jupiter	expand with devotion
♄	Saturn	control modestly
♅	Uranus	invent mysteriously
♆	Neptune	inspire fascinatingly
♇	Pluto	transform privately

The aspects

Events in life do not happen in isolation. What occurs in one area has a bearing on others. This is reflected by the way that the planets make angular relationships to each other. Some aspects indicate easy flows of energy; others more difficult flows. Both possibilities together create the opportunities of our lives. Below are the symbols, degree separations, names and meanings of the main aspects.

☌	0	Conjunction	varies with planets
⊻	30	Semi-sextile	mildly friendly
□	45	Semi-square	somewhat stressful
✳	60	Sextile	friendly
□	90	Square	very stressful
△	120	Trine	very harmonious
□	135	Sesqui-square	awkward
⊼	150	Quincunx	strain
☍	180	Opposition	confronting

Putting it all together

Now we have all the elements to interpret more fully. By focusing upon each outer-planetary archetype in its sign of the time and then combining these planets and signs, we can assess the forces of any time. This gives vital insights into historical change and helps us to anticipate the future.

How to find out more

The fuller appendix in *Astrology and Compassion the Convenient Truth* offers a beginning in natal and other branches of astrology. Astrology is both a science and an art. The calculations and the key meanings that relate to each concept are scientifically precise, but the depth of interpretation and conclusions arrived at by juxtaposing the images is an art.

We become more proficient with astrology by using it. 'Suck it and see', we used to say when I was a boy. By comparing history to astro-cycles do you understand history better? If you learn about full horoscope charts and try to interpret them, does this make the people, institutions and events they represent clearer? Let your developing experience be the way to learn.

A good professional astrologer will have considered tens of thousands of charts and developed methods too varied to be explained here. A good astrologer will also have much more experience of the myriad ways the cycles combine at each unique moment of time.

To help you improve your understanding by tapping into this knowledge, below is just a small selection of beginners' resources.

A book with a chart calculator tool to teach yourself

The serious astrologer will wish to learn how to construct a horoscope and build up interpretation skills.

My book *The Secret Language of Astrology* is a beautifully illustrated introduction to astrology's concepts and methods. It is linked to a website [http://secretlanguageofastrology.com/], which will calculate birth and present astro-cycle charts. By using this integrated tool alone, first-time readers can interpret themselves and see astrology working.

More books

At the end of the chapters of my *Astrology and Compassion the Convenient Truth* are lists of key books in shops and online.

Software possibilities

To learn thoroughly, taking classes with a recognised astrological school is the best way — see information below.

Initially, however, computer technology makes it possible start advancing your understanding of the basics of astrology.

Solar Fire computer software performs the calculations and helps with the interpretation. It created the charts in this book. Astrolabe Inc publishes it worldwide. Their site also offers a free natal chart generation service. Visit: http://www.alabe.com.

Astro Gold is a simplified app. for the I-phone and android mobile systems.

Below are additional contacts:

http://www.astro.com offers information and a chart service

http://www.astrosoftware.com for Kepler/Matrix software

http://www.timecycles.com for Io Macintosh software

Classes, consultations and organisations
Lists of schools are to be found in the web sites below. If you do not wish to study but want to find out more about yourself, consulting a professional astrologer can be most beneficial and liberating, when full expertise and experience can be focused on your present situation and future.

The sites below give links to consultants and classes:
http://www.astrologicalassociation.com
http:// www.uraniatrust.org
http://www.isarastrology.com
http://www.astrologer.com/metalog
http://www.professionalastrologers.org

Notes

[1] Saturn was opposing Pluto across the Ascendant/Descendant of the US Declaration of Independence chart, and then both planets were to conjunct or oppose its massive 7th/8th house stellium for a decade or more. [US 'Sibley' chart - 1650 LMT 4 July 1776 Philadelphia PA]

[2] Just ahead was an opposition between Jupiter and Neptune in Leo/Aquarius, near to a key degree in the foundation chart for the modern-day Middle East.[1122 CEDT 25 April 1920 San Remo Italy]

[3] For a full explanation of the astrology of these times and the leaders that drove the agenda, see Chapter 5 of *Astrology and Compassion the Convenient Truth* by Roy Gillett ISBN 978-1-906154-07-3 – especially pages 82-8.

[4] Ibid.

[5] For example in his evidence the Treasury Select Committee of the British House of Commons 'It is always possible to set policy with the benefit of hindsight... there is no way in which the committee can have perfect foresight.' Quoted on 12th November 2008 in http://www.ldpbusiness.co.uk/liverpool-news/liverpool-business-news/2008/11/12/bank-of-england-says-2009-economy-could-contract-by-2-96026-22242017/

[6] Ibid Chapter 14.

[7] Ibid Chapters 5 and 7.

[8] *Cycles of Becoming* by Alexander Ruperti.

[9] *Cosmos and Psyche* by Richard Tarnas.

[10] This booklet assumes a basic understanding and experience of astrology. Readers not familiar with the subject will find the Appendix starting on page 101 most useful. For a full introduction, readers are referred to *Astrology and Compassion the Convenient Truth by* Roy Gillett for an introduction to its workings, answers to astrology's critics and many examples of its value in personal and social life.

[11] It is not suggested that Pluto or any other planet has a direct effect, but rather that a planet's moving position can be used as a reference point from which to measure each stage of a cycle. This cycle may be the combined effects of many factors. It is ironic that Pluto should be downgraded to a dwarf planet by astronomers just 18 months before its cycle was to suggest very real economic change.

[12] As well as background information for general economic planning, astro-cycles have been used by hard-working technical minds to project specific price movements and levels, and even company performance. Chapter 15 of *Astrology and Compassion the Convenient Truth* introduces the methods and gives further reading bibliography from the experts in this field. The overlap between the limitation and

ethical foundation of this expertise would be a worthy subject for discussion on another occasion.

[13] http://en.wikipedia.org/wiki/South_Sea_Company

[14] Hansard, House of Lords, 5th series, vol. 468, cols. 390-1.

[15] 1993 US Presidential Inauguration chart 1200 EST 20 January 1993 Washington DC

[16] The US 'Sibley' chart - 1650 LMT 4 July 1776 Philadelphia PA

[17] The reaction of politicians and the public to the news of economic disaster seems to have followed the five stages of reaction to grief outlined in *On Death and Dying* by Elisabeth Kübler-Ross.

[18] Report from China by Paul Mason, BBC *Newsnight* 17 June 2009.

[19] For full details see 'Working with the Planets' *Astrological Journal* Vol50 No 3 (May/June 2009)

[20] The full horoscope of the morning on the day of the opening of the meeting is printed on page 103 in the Appendix of this study.

[21] Gordon Brown was born 0840 UT 20 February 1951 Griffnock, Scotland

[22] Barack Obama was born 1924 AHST 4th August 1961 Honolulu Hawaii

[23] Not necessarily meaning advice from young people, but rather counsel coming from an immature understanding of the background.

[24] Regulus entered the sign Leo of the tropical zodiac in 157 BC

[25] Chiron is often held to represent the qualities of its mythological archetype to learn and be healed by experiencing our own wounds. Neptune is the joint ruler of Pisces, the sign it is about to enter for only the second time since its discovery in on 23 September 1846. It is held to represent spiritual, artistic and confusingly seductive experiences. The Pre-Raphaelite and magical developments in the second half of the 19th century could be explained by its discovery in these artists birth charts and then its conjunction to Pluto in 1890/92.

[26] In his book *The Great Year,* Nicholas Campion studied in depth the wish of some human beings to live at *the* end of days. In his *Book of World Horoscopes* he lists 95 dates between 1457 and 3550 AD, when the Age of Aquarius was claimed to commence.

[27] The recent example of British Members of Parliament, even government ministers and front bench opposition members, justifying the claiming a wide range of expenses for two homes, while renting out a third on the grounds that they were 'acting within the rules', shows how ineffective and economically wasteful relying on rules can be when there is no will to do what is efficient and ethically correct.

[28] Franklin Roosevelt became President of the USA in 1933, two and a half years after the cardinal T-square. The market bottomed in July 1932. Barack Obama became President in 2009 at a time when the market was struggling to find a bottom and 18 months before the July 2010 grand cross.

[29] 'For anything we take, an equal amount must be given in some way' –see Chapter 1 — especially pages 19/20.

[30] 'Villanelle for our Time' *Leonard Cohen, Dear Heather*. Readers are encouraged to obtain the *Dear Heather* album and listen to Leonard's sensitive full reading of this most perceptive poem.

[31] http://startacellphonebusiness.com/articles/when-was-the-first-mobile-phone-invented-.html

[32] http://www.networkworld.com/community/node/21418

[33] Many suggestions that this was to occur at the 20th/21st century changeover were based on a simplistic interpretation of the calendar's relationship to the second to third millennium of the Christian era. The Uranus/Neptune focus upon Aquarius during the changeover period may have encouraged such a view.

[34] The computer search was between 5,00BC and 2,500 AD. Only in 2009 and 2485 are the three bodies together in Aquarius.

[35] Obtainable at http://www.crucialastrotools.co.uk or your usual bookseller

[36] There are a number of systems that associate planets and zodiac signs with particular stones, colour, planets, and so on. These lists are not complete in every category. Also some alternative associations may be found to be more suitable for some astrological systems. These ideas are just to get you started. You are encouraged to check up and research further.

NOW READ THE VITAL 2017 sequel to
Economy Ecology and Kindness.

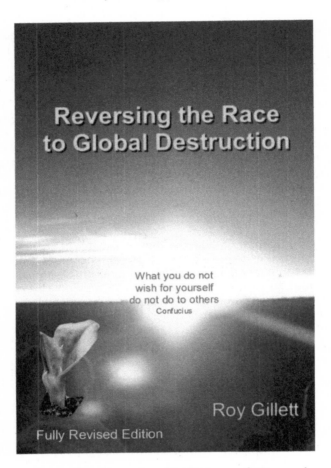

Abandoning the Politics of Greed
Offers detailed radical answers to today's economic and
social problems.

Available in all E-book formats and hard copy at all
shop and online outlets, author-signed copies.
email: crucialbooks@virginmedia.com
http://crucialbooks.co.uk/

Then read and use the other two invaluable books in...

Roy Gillett's Astrological Quartet

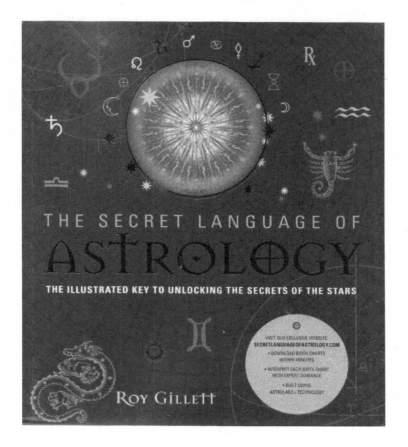

Beautifully designed full colour volume, to help you
learn astrology from the beginning or be a
companion to show friends and enhance your work.

———————————————————————————————————

E-book: http://www.secretlanguageofastrology.com
Hard copy: all shop and online outlets, author-signed
copies email: cruicalbooks@virginmedia.com
http://crucialbooks.co.uk/

Astrology & Compassion
the Convenient Truth

Roy Gillett

Know the real nature of astrology and its potential to benefit conventional academia and help clarify society's legal, financial, social and learning problems.

Printed in July 2021
by Rotomail Italia S.p.A., Vignate (MI) - Italy